JCSS Study no. 18

The Dynamics of Soviet Policy in the Middle East: Between Old Thinking and New

Mark A. Heller

First published 1991 by Westview Press, Inc.

Published 2019 by Routledge
52 Vanderbilt Avenue, New York, NY 10017
2 Park Square, Milton Park, Abingdon, Oxon OX14 4RN

Routledge is an imprint of the Taylor & Francis Group, an informa business

Library of Congress Cataloging-in-Publication Data

Heller, Mark.
The dynamics of Soviet policy in the Middle East / Mark A. Heller.
p. cm. -- (JCSS study ; no. 18)
ISBN 0-8133-1415-1
1. Middle East--Foreign relations--Soviet Union. 2. Soviet Union--Foreign relations--Middle East. 3. Soviet Union--Foreign relations--1985-1991. I. Title. II. Series.
DS63.2.S65D96 1992
327.47056--dc20 92-27567
CIP

ISBN 13: 978-0-367-29141-9 (hbk)
ISBN 13: 978-0-367-30687-8 (pbk)

The Jaffee Center for Strategic Studies (JCSS)

The Center for Strategic Studies was established at Tel Aviv University at the end of 1977. In 1983 it was named the Jaffee Center for Strategic Studies in honor of Mr. and Mrs. Mel Jaffee. The objective of the Center is to contribute to the expansion of knowledge on strategic subjects and to promote public understanding of and pluralistic thought on matters of national and international security.

The Center relates to the concept of strategy in its broadest meaning, namely, the complex of processes involved in the identification, mobilization and application of resources in peace and war, in order to solidify and strengthen national and international security.

International Board of Trustees

Table of Contents

Preface

The text of this study was essentially completed at the end of 1990 and slightly updated in the spring of 1991 to reflect the course of the Gulf War. Soviet behavior before and during the fighting confirmed both the basic thrust of changing Middle Eastern policy implicit in new thinking and the impact of the remaining impediments to its thoroughgoing implementation.

The most serious of these impediments was the resistance of conservative forces, whose world-view, self-image and institutional interests were threatened by new thinking in domestic as well as foreign and national security policy, of which the Middle East was but one component. This inseparable link between the domestic and foreign dimensions of new thinking was dramatically illustrated during the abortive coup d'etat of August 1991 which was publicly welcomed (apart from unrepentant communists) only by Iraq, Libya and elements of the PLO — precisely those foreign actors who had once benefited so much from Soviet old thinking. The failure of the putsch finally cleared away this obstacle and made it possible to accelerate the movement of Soviet policy along the path logically dictated by the requirements of restructuring, which had already been apparent for several years.

The restoration of ambassadorial-level diplomatic relations with Israel in October 1991 was not itself a result of the failed coup, since it coincided with Israel's decision to attend an international peace conference and therefore conformed with longstanding Soviet policy. But other actions after August, including the long-delayed implementation of a civil aviation agreement calling for direct flights and the hosting of Israeli visitors at previously-closed military facilities, indicated that all Soviet inhibitions about cultivating close ties with Israel had disappeared. Indeed, so completely had traditional patterns been overturned that Israelis seemed no less favorably disposed than Arabs to Soviet participation in the peace conference, and perhaps even more so.

The irony, of course, is that by this time, Soviet involvement could not denote coequal status with the United States and was scarcely relevant for any of the other protagonists, because the failed coup had also accelerated the ongoing decline of Soviet influence abroad and the disintegrating power of the central government at home. During Mikhail Gorbachev's brief visit to the Madrid peace conference in October 1991, few journalists were interested in his views on the Arab-Israeli peace process; most wanted to know whether he still wielded any authority over the fractious and self-assertive republics at home. Indeed, his presence at the conference seemed mostly a matter of noblesse oblige, a gesture by President Bush to a man who had set in motion momentous changes which then passed him by. For the foreseeable future, the great imponderable was not the course of Soviet Middle Eastern policy, but whether the Soviet Union, beset by seemingly insurmountable domestic problems, would continue to exist at all.

In preparing this study, I benefited greatly from discussions with scholars and government officials in Israel, the Soviet Union and the United States. I am also grateful to my colleagues at the Jaffee Center for Strategic Studies and to two anonymous reviewers for their comments and criticisms of earlier drafts of the text. For any errors of fact or interpretation, I remain solely responsible.

M.A.H.
November 1, 1991

Summary

Since the accession to power of Mikhail Gorbachev in 1985, the Soviet Union has been undergoing a transformation of revolutionary proportions. The major impetus for this change was a crisis of the Soviet system, reflected in protracted economic stagnation. However, the Soviet leadership under Gorbachev has recognized that the successful restructuring of the economy depends, not only on political democratization at home, but also on the end of ruinously expensive arms races and the mobilization of economic and technical assistance from abroad, and these, in turn, require the relaxation of international tensions. Accordingly, the Soviets have elaborated a set of principles — new political thinking — to guide foreign policy. Militarized, ideologized competition with the forces of imperialism has been abandoned in favor of cooperation in the peaceful resolution of disputes. New political thinking has meant that the Soviet Union no longer views the Third World as an arena for a zero-sum superpower competition for influence and presence. Rather than seeking sterile political or ideological gains at American expense, it now seeks to eliminate friction with the United States stemming from Third World commitments and to commercialize and universalize its foreign relations, regardless of ideological considerations.

Insofar as the Middle East is concerned, the application of new thinking has meant a reduction in Soviet political, economic and military support for radical forces and the cultivation of better ties with "pro-western" states. The most dramatic change has taken place in the Soviet approach to Israel: legal and administrative constraints on emigration by Soviet Jews have disappeared, leading to a flood of Soviet immigration to Israel, and bilateral relations have been fully normalized except for the formal restoration of diplomatic ties (which appears to be merely a matter of time). But Soviet behavior has changed in other respects, as well; diplomatic cooperation with the United States in opposing the Iraqi invasion of Kuwait and participation in the arms embargo and economic sanctions against Iraq would have been virtually unthinkable before 1985.

The principles of new political thinking have not been applied with complete consistency. Vestiges of old thinking, including the slow pace of normalization with Israel, continued military ties with Syria, and competitive policies during the Iran-Iraq War, are explained by a variety of factors: inertia, domestic politics (bureaucratic interests, lingering conservatism, and the growing assertiveness of Soviet Muslims), irrationality (especially anti-Semitism), and American provocations. Moreover, some practices, such as commercial sales of conventional arms, may have a destabilizing impact but are characteristic of almost every "normal" state and are unlikely to change in the future.

For 30 years after 1955, competitive superpower involvement posed a constant danger that Middle Eastern conflicts would escalate into a direct superpower confrontation, perhaps leading to war. New thinking appears to have eliminated that danger. But its impact on the Middle East itself is far more equivocal. The withdrawal of Soviet backing for various clients may cause them to be more cautious about resorting to military force. Indeed, by depriving them of important resources for confrontation, it may induce them to consider possibilities for political conciliation previously rejected. On the other hand, the most important factors in such decisions have always been immediate political needs and the local military balance; the Soviets were never very effective in restraining their allies, their new thinking has no immediate impact on the political needs of local powers, and arms sales — at least of conventional weapons — are likely to continue on a commercial basis. Moreover, the reduced risk of superpower confrontation may also reduce the incentive of the superpowers to make large investments of time and resources in order to promote settlements of the Arab-Israeli and other Middle Eastern conflicts. And whatever their incentive may be, the Soviets have very few assets to contribute to conflict resolution efforts.

For Israel, the most profound consequence of Soviet new thinking is the massive immigration of Soviet Jews. In other respects, and especially in questions of war and peace, Soviet policy is likely to be more constructive, but it is not yet clear that this will make a decisive difference. The most important outside power for Israel and the rest of the Middle East will continue to be the United States. In the last analysis, however, the key to the future of all people in the Middle East ultimately rests, as always, in their own hands.

Chapter 1. The Third World in Soviet Policy

Since the accession to power of Mikhail Gorbachev in 1985, the familiar contours of post-war history have changed, in many cases beyond all recognition. The image of the Soviet Union as a stolid, totalitarian communist regime has been challenged by cultural effervescence, efforts to restructure the economic system, the liberalization of Party and government politics, and the growing drive for autonomy or independence by the various nationalities of the Soviet Union. The image of the Soviet Union as a militaristic global power determined to maintain its sphere of influence at any cost and to expand it through subversion or violence has been challenged by reforms in Soviet force structure and military doctrine, acquiescence in the overthrow of communist regimes in Eastern Europe and the reunification of Germany, the dissolution of the Warsaw Pact, the withdrawal from Afghanistan, and a declared posture of international cooperation to resolve regional conflicts by political means.

Since the character and behavior of the Soviet Union have an impact on practically every facet of international politics and security, these changes have provoked the most fundamental and far-reaching debate since the onset of the Cold War. Indeed, Soviet terminology for these phenomena — glasnost (the opening up of information and expression), perestroika (restructuring of the political and economic systems), and novoye mishleniye ("new thinking" in the principles guiding the behavior of the Soviet government at home and abroad) — have been incorporated into the lexicon of international discourse. At the highest level of generality, the changes associated with Gorbachev have created a sense of revolutionary transformation. However, the outcome of this process is by no means predetermined, because the Soviet leadership itself may lose control or lose confidence in its chosen course (as the resignation of Foreign Minister Edward Shevardnadze in December 1990 clearly suggested). Much uncertainty remains about the direction, pace and durability of change, and about its ultimate meaning for other actors in the international system. This is particularly true with respect to Soviet behavior in the Third World and its impact on regional instabilities and bilateral Soviet-American relations.

The purpose of this study is to examine the extent to which new political thinking has been applied to Soviet policy in the Middle East and to speculate about the possible impact of any changes on patterns of international relations in the region. The Middle East should be a particularly revealing test case of Soviet new thinking. Of all Third World regions, it is the closest geographically, it has attracted the greatest Soviet investment in recent decades, it is potentially the most closely linked to Soviet domestic politics, and its economic and strategic importance have historically given crises and conflicts there the greatest resonance in global politics and bilateral Soviet-American relations. Indeed, Middle Eastern exceptions to overall Soviet policy may be logically required by the exceptional character of the region. However, thoroughgoing changes in Soviet policy in the Middle East would, precisely because of that region's importance, constitute prima facie evidence that the entire basis of the Soviet approach to the Third World had been profoundly shaken.

Expansionism has been the hallmark of Soviet foreign policy and of the Russian Empire before it. Unlike other European great powers, however, the Russian tradition is one of expansion at the margins. Russian Czars sought cultural and economic influence wherever they could, but the extension of Romanov political-military control generally meant the sustained overland expansion of the state borders, rather than the acquisition of farflung overseas possessions. Whenever a countervailing force was encountered at the frontier of Russian power, state policy was to undermine the influence and presence of the competing power center: Austria in the southwest, Sweden and Poland in the northwest, China in the east, Turkey and Persia in the south, and Britain in India and the Middle East.

There is nothing exceptional about such behavior. On the contrary, it conforms with the tendency of every actor in an anarchical international system, whether for offensive or defensive reasons, to push out the range of its influence to the maximum extent permitted by its resources, and there is therefore no need to look for explanations peculiar to the Russian people or the character of their government. Nevertheless, national identities and political ideologies do influence the policies of governments in the sense that they shape geographical priorities and modes of action, provide rationales, and help determine the choice and effectiveness of various foreign policy instruments.

The Bolshevik Revolution provided an ideological reason, or at least rationale, for Soviet involvement throughout the world. Communism was held to be a socio-economic doctrine of universal applicability, and Soviet efforts to help extend it were both required by the logic of history and necessary for the security of the Soviet state — the embodiment of the Revolution — against the forces of imperialism determined to overthrow it. Contrary to Marx's prediction, capitalism had persisted in the advanced, industrial countries long after it reached its monopoly stage and the explanation, according to Lenin, lay in imperialism.

> ...instead of having developed its internal contradictions and tensions to a point where a revolutionary break must occur, capitalism has found a way out of these contradictions.... The way out is expansion into the whole world in search of cheap raw materials, ready markets for commodities and for excess capital, and most important, cheap labor.... This expansion of capitalism is called imperialism. By embarking on it, capitalism has, for the time being, staved off the revolution and its own downfall.[1]

With the superprofits gained from exploiting the underdeveloped countries, capitalists were able to bribe labor leaders and "the upper stratum of the labor aristocracy" in their own countries, and thereby ensure their own survival.[2]

In this analysis, overseas colonies are the weak link in the chain that sustains capitalism. If the link can be broken by disconnecting the colonies from their metropolises, then the imperialist powers themselves will be weakened to the point where they will not only be unable to throttle the socialist revolution in its Soviet cradle, but will themselves also become ripe for revolution at home. However, it was not at all clear that the political dissolution of empires would be sufficient to produce these results. National liberation movements might achieve political independence but still leave their countries closely integrated into the global network of capitalism, thus perpetuating the economic dynamics of imperialism under a new guise: neo-colonialism. Much depended on the class structure and domestic policies pursued by the leaders of formerly dependent countries. The collapse of the European and Japanese colonial empires after World War II imparted a worldwide dimension and political immediacy to this problem, but it was one with which Soviet theoreticians and policymakers had had to grapple since the first years of post-revolution foreign policy: "What is the correct Soviet approach to nationalist, non-communist liberation movements and governments?"

Soviet policy in the Third World has been periodized in a variety of ways, but however many "stages" observers may count, the major variable appears to be movement along the scale of responses to this basic question, with the two poles being almost exclusive identification with and support for orthodox communists, at one end, and virtually indiscriminate identification with and support for any forces hostile to the major imperialist powers, at the other.[3] As part of a general "relaxation" which accompanied the transition from War Communism to the New Economic Plan, Lenin himself legitimized the second approach by endorsing temporary alliances with the bourgeois leadership of nationalist movements and of governments in the developing countries of Asia, Africa and Latin America. "Socialists," he wrote, "must not only demand the unconditional and immediate liberation of the colonies without compensation...but they must render determined support to the more revolutionary elements in the bourgeois-democratic movements...and assist their uprising — and, if need be, their revolutionary war — against the imperialist powers that oppress them."[4] This position was criticized by more dogmatic Marxists such as the Indian Communist M.N. Roy, who insisted that revolutionary national movements would not really succeed under bourgeois leadership and that "leadership would have to be taken over by the communist parties when the bourgeoisie deserted and betrayed the national revolution, as they were bound to do."[5] Since bourgeois leaders were expected either to compromise in the struggle for independence or to settle for the trappings of political independence while leaving imperial economic ties essentially intact, communist support for them was expected to be at best futile, if not self-defeating.

However, it was Lenin's view that prevailed. It is true that efforts were made to enhance the ideological and institutional authority of the Soviet leadership over the national movements. For example, the Fourth Comintern Congress proclaimed, in the *Theses on the Eastern Question*, "It is one of the most important functions of the anti-imperialist united front tactic to make clear to the broad working masses the necessity of an alliance with the international proletariat and the Soviet republics."[6] Nevertheless, this was not a major determinant of Soviet state behavior. Lenin established the diplomatic practice of offering sympathy and support to unequivocally bourgeois or even feudal nativist movements and regimes in such countries as Turkey, Persia and Afghanistan, because in their political struggles against the domination of the main imperial power on the Soviet periphery — Great Britain — they were playing an objectively anti-imperialist role. In short, Lenin bequeathed to his successors both a conceptual framework for the struggle against imperialist powers to be played out over the entire world, and a clear appreciation of the advantages to be gained in that struggle by properly manipulating the forces of nationalism among non-European peoples.

However, the credibility of this tendency was seriously undermined in 1927-28 by the "treason" of the Soviet-support Kuomintang Party in China and the nearly mortal blow it inflicted on the Chinese Communist Party. Until then, Stalin had essentially pursued Lenin's approach to the question of national-liberation, thereby allying himself on foreign as well as domestic issues with Bukharin and other "rightist" forces. Indeed, the issue was an additional point of contention in Stalin's struggle for power with Trotsky. Stalin favored alliance with and support of the national bourgeoisie, provided that it objectively served the cause of anti-imperialism (as Kuomintang opposition to British interests in China apparently did). Proletarian support, he urged, "must be given to those national movements which tend to weaken imperialism and bring about the overthrow of imperialism, and not to strengthen and preserve it."[7] Following the setback in China, Stalin eliminated Trotsky but then turned on his erstwhile allies, led by Bukharin, and adopted the harder theoretical line advocated by Trotsky and before that by Roy.

The new logic, incidentally, was also applied to communist parties in Europe, which avoided making common cause with other anti-fascist forces until the growing power of Nazi Germany presented an immediate and unambiguous threat to Soviet security. In the mid-1930s, European communist parties were directed to join various "Popular Fronts" in order to forestall the further progress of fascism, and communist parties in the Third World suppressed their revolutionary instincts in order not to distract the imperial powers from the main task, which was to resist Germany and Japan. But insofar as direct Soviet interest in the Third World was concerned, the communist liberation movement remained a dead letter for more than 20 years.[8]

Contrary to common perception, postwar policy under Stalin was not uniformly rigid. It is true that Soviet policy in the Third World between 1945 and 1953 was generally marked by a low profile, due to weakness and the need to concentrate on reconstruction, higher priorities elsewhere (especially in Europe itself), and what one observer has termed "ideological myopia."[9] Soviet leaders viewed the world in dichotomous terms — capitalist and socialist — and in accordance with the so-called "two camps doctrine" associated with the name of Andrei Zhdanov, rejected any cooperation with or support for the national bourgeoisie in the national-liberation movements. Even during this first Cold War phase, however, the Soviet Union assisted certain non-communist forces which appeared to threaten imperialist interests; support for the creation of Israel was a noteworthy example of such behavior. Even in this case, however, Soviet reading of the class character of the forces involved played an important role; the Soviets assumed that the feudal or bourgeois Arab regimes opposing Israel were, by definition, serving British interests in the Middle East. By and large, ideological prisms produced indifference to, or active suspicion of national-liberation movements by both Soviet spokesmen and local communists; denunciations of

Gandhi and the Congress in India are a case in point.

However, this hard, exclusivist line effectively prevented any broadening of the mass base of communist parties and led to serious setbacks for those parties, especially in Asia. Just as importantly, it prevented Soviet adaptation to a rapidly-changing world of independent states in the former colonial areas. In 1949, communists were therefore instructed to bid for the support of that part of the national bourgeoisie "that suffered from foreign competition" and to pay special attention to the peasantry.[10] This reorientation, no doubt inspired by the success of the Chinese Communist Party, was still a partial one. There was as yet no recognition that a national revolution under bourgeois leadership might mean real independence for a former colony. Before these countries could be helped to play their assigned role of weakening imperialism, Soviet policy had first to admit the possibility that non-communist leaders could be anything other than western stooges, and this required further modification of the "two camps" doctrine. By 1951, there were already indications of a reevaluation of the possibility of using expanded trade and economic aid as a weapon to drive a wedge between the West and the newly-independent underdeveloped countries, and at the 19th Congress of the Communist Party of the Soviet Union (CPSU) in 1952, a new policy was formally announced.[11]

Thus, the foundations for a reintroduction of Leninist principles into Soviet relations with the Third World were actually laid under Stalin. A truly active Third World policy, however, was only instituted after 1953, when Nikita Khrushchev entrenched this "new-old" approach and the usefulness of national self-determination as an instrument to weaken the West was reinforced by the example of swift Soviet reconstruction and modernization. Of course, the opportunities for more tangible gains also increased. The disintegration of the British, French and Belgian overseas empires during Khrushchev's tenure and the post-independence resentments and weaknesses of many former colonies left little doubt that an anti-western animus existed which could potentially be exploited to Soviet advantage, provided sufficient ideological and diplomatic flexibility were forthcoming. In particular, the widespread desire for neutralism or non-alignment in the Cold War, symbolized by the convening of the Bandung Conference in 1955, indicated that the bourgeois leadership of these countries did intend to distance itself from the West and play a far more "progressive" role in international relations than Soviet leaders had previously thought possible.

At the 20th Party Congress in 1956, Khrushchev therefore focused his attention on the vast "zone of peace" made up of nonaligned, underdeveloped nations. The central themes in Soviet relations with these states were henceforth to be peaceful coexistence and benevolent noninterference, demonstrated by generous trade and aid agreements. In a sense, the Soviet leadership resolved to compete with the West for the support of these states by offering an alternative source of developmental assistance, thereby enabling them to do what they were in any event predisposed to do, that is, to loosen their ties with the West. In the following years, the guiding principle was "that these new states, although state capitalist and part of the world capitalist system, occupied a special place within that system, reflected in their neutral foreign policy and their desire for economic independence. Thus, they had a special status, marking a progressive stage on the road to socialism."[12]

Nothing in this policy was meant to imply that the Soviet Union or communist parties loyal to it had abandoned all interest in the class character of regimes in developing countries or all desire to see the ultimate triumph of socialism. Indeed, much effort was invested in endowing Soviet-supported and -aligned countries with ideological legitimacy. Lacking guidance from the corpus of classical Marxism, Soviet ideologues created new categories of analysis. The most notable of these was the progressive, postliberation "national-democratic state," endorsed at the Moscow Conference of 81 Communist Parties in December 1960 and codified at the 22nd CPSU Congress in 1961. The national democracy was defined as:

> a state which consistently upholds its political and economic independence, fights against imperialism and its military blocs, and against military bases on its territory; a state which fights against the new forms of colonialism and the penetration of imperialistic capital; a state which rejects

> dictatorial and despotic forms of government; a state in which the people are assured broad democratic rights and freedoms (freedom of speech, press, assembly, demonstrations, establishment of political parties and public organizations), the opportunity to work for the enactment of an agrarian reform and the realization of other democratic and social changes and for participation in shaping government policy.[13]

Such formulations professed to derive from a scientific understanding of socio-economic forces, such as the putative contradiction between the interests of the national bourgeoisie and those of imperialism, but the terms used left much latitude for subjective interpretation and were sufficiently elastic to provide ideological justification for relations with virtually any state in the Third World prepared to act or speak against western interests. Ideology was not ignored, but rather than a determinant of policy (which it had never really been) or even a tool for understanding the world in which Soviet decisionmakers had to operate, it was increasingly becoming a method of ex post facto rationalization for policies pursued for other reasons, primarily, the desire to undermine the position of the West (which by this time essentially meant the United States), and to enhance Soviet presence and influence, sought as ends in themselves.

During most of the late 1950s and early 1960s, the Soviet policy of providing undifferentiated encouragement of and support for anti-western nationalist forces paid handsome dividends. Starting from a virtually non-existent base, Soviet diplomacy was able to reap large returns from fairly small investments. Charismatic Third World leaders, influenced either by leftist parties in their former metropolises or by the dominant intellectual currents in the western universities where many of them studied, opted for a statist economic regime at home and a strident anti-western foreign policy. Economic and educational ties were established with the Soviet Union, resulting in a growing Soviet presence in these countries and a constant rise in the number of Third World trainees and students in the Soviet Union or Eastern European countries. In international affairs, the general tendency among these leaders was to endorse Soviet positions in the Cold War confrontation with the United States. Among the individuals associated with these trends were the leading personalities of the non-aligned movement: Sukarno in Indonesia, Kwame Nkrumah in Ghana, Modibo Keita in Mali, Sekou Toure in Guinea, Abd al-Nasir in Egypt, Tito (despite his historic split with Stalin) in Yugoslavia, and even, to some extent, Nehru in India.

By the mid-1960s, however, developments had revealed important inadequacies in this approach and produced considerable disillusionment. The most important change was that the Soviet Union, as it began to acquire assets in the Third World, also began to appreciate the shortcomings of its allies in terms of both durability and reliability. Many of the luminaries upon whom its initial gains depended were exposed as weak reeds on which to lean. In some countries, the nationalist credentials of such leaders as Sukarno, Nkrumah, and Keita, as well as Patrice Lumumba in Zaire and Ahmad Ben Bella in Algeria, were not enough to prevent their ouster in military or factional coups. In others, non-alignment was interpreted seriously enough to permit various regimes to cultivate economic ties with both blocs, and in a competition based on trade and aid, the Soviet Union was not necessarily well-positioned to win. Finally, even in those cases where a combination of anti-western nationalism and great need permitted the entrenchment of Soviet influence, as in Egypt, the result was often a hugely expensive Soviet commitment, the political payoffs of which were frequently ephemeral and always fragile. Egypt's massive indebtedness, for example, was not a reliable instrument of leverage, since, as Abd al-Nasir himself argued, "An indebted person has only to refuse to pay if he feels that unjust pressure is being put on him."[14] In short, bourgeois nationalist regimes were proving to be unreliable or insufficiently anti-imperialist, and the efficiency and efficacy of Soviet policy — which had essentially been to facilitate the rupture of those regimes' ties with the West by providing an alternate economic model and source of assistance — were increasingly dubious.

Following Khrushchev's ouster by Leonid Brezhnev and his clique in 1964, Soviet Third World policy entered a phase of what Fukuyama has called "moribund Khrushchevism," meaning a continuing focus on the cultivation of anti-western regimes and movements, but a palpable shift to reliance on instruments which enhanced the dependency of recipients and in which the Soviet Union had a greater comparative advantage: weapons, advisers, technicians, and other forms of military assistance.[15] In effect, bourgeois nationalism remained the point d'appui of Soviet involvement, but with less enthusiasm and optimism (or naivete) about the prospects for revolutionary transformation and less generosity in the relationship.[16] The major shift was from economic assistance and exhortation/instruction about non-capitalist paths to development, to a more militarized approach. Thus, Soviet economic aid to non-communist Third World countries was at least equal to the value of military assistance from the mid-1950s to the mid-1960s, averaging about $380 million per annum between 1955 and 1964; some sources state or imply that it was even greater.[17] In the following decade, however, arms transfers were at least double the value of economic aid; economic aid agreements averaged about $625 million, but average annual arms transfer agreements came to $1.5 billion, and even actual deliveries were about $1.0 billion.[18] This shift produced tangible results in terms of the strategic payoffs — greater military presence, access to bases and facilities — but these payoffs did not necessarily prove to be more enduring than in the past. Some "allied" regimes continued to exploit the superpower competition by appealing to both superpowers; some went even further and simply defected.

During the second half of the Brezhnev era, Soviet Third World policy passed into what has been called the "Khomeini period."[19] Beginning roughly in the mid-1970s, two major features marked Soviet policy: a much more active use of military instruments, particularly direct intervention by Soviet or surrogate forces, and a renewed emphasis on ideological factors, especially the revolutionary character of Soviet partners or proteges. These changes did not entail an abrupt and complete renunciation of previous patterns. The Soviets continued to deal with established bourgeois nationalist clients, and the salience of military components in the overall aid-and-trade package continued to grow, at an accelerating pace. The decade 1975-1984 roughly corresponds with this period (although there were, as we shall see, indications of a reassessment soon after Brezhnev's death, and to some extent even before). During that decade, economic assistance agreements with non-communist developing countries amounted to about $7.15 billion, whereas military aid and trade came to almost $75 billion, i.e., more than ten times as much.[20] However, arms transfers during this period were also increasingly viewed as a mechanism for raising hard currency to cover the trade deficits incurred as a result of massive imports of grain from western countries. Consequently, the prices for Soviet weapons were raised, financing terms were far less generous than in the past, and the geographic emphasis shifted to countries, especially in the Middle East, who could pay hard currency for their purchases. As a result, by the mid-1980s almost 80 percent of military deliveries to the Third World were hard currency transactions, and arms sales accounted for 25-30 percent of total hard currency revenues, as opposed to about 3 percent in the early 1970s.[21]

In short, the Soviets did not abandon the tools previously used to establish and entrench their political and diplomatic influence. Nevertheless, they relied much more on two other instruments. The first — military intervention — was not entirely new to the Soviet Third World policy repertoire; Soviet pilots had taken part in the Yemen War in the late 1960s and air defense forces intervened on a large scale in the Israeli-Egyptian War of Attrition in 1970. However, the 1970s saw both qualitative and quantitative breakthroughs, in the sense that Soviet or surrogate forces were sent, not only to defend established clients, but also to move the front-lines in ongoing conflicts and help determine their outcome, i.e., to change the status quo. The second tool — support for Marxist-Leninist liberation movements or regimes and attempts to convert them into vanguard parties committed to scientific socialism — was as old as the Bolshevik Revolution itself.

In neither case was the choice of instrument solely the result of greater intellectual insight. The utility of the first stemmed from several changes in the global balance of power. One was simply an impressive growth in Soviet power projection capabilities. The accumulation of staging areas and the major buildup of conventional military strength under Brezhnev endowed the Soviet Union with far greater air- and sea-lift capabilities and forces appropriate for rapid intervention than it had ever had before. This change coincided with the emergence of significant constraints on American intervention capabilities; the years after Vietnam witnessed an atrophy of US power and the will to use it, of which the most prominent symbol was the Clark Amendment of 1975, whereby Congress prohibited assistance to any Angolan rebels. Soviet decisionmakers, though normally cautious about direct intervention, were therefore less inhibited about using military force. Finally, local circumstances during this period, especially the disintegration of the Portuguese colonial empire in Africa and domestic revolutions in Ethiopia and Afghanistan, held out apparent opportunities for significant political gains from relatively small but timely applications of military force.[22] As a result, this decade witnessed several instances of military intervention outside the Soviet Bloc, most notably in Angola, Ethiopia, and Afghanistan.

The second change was a reflection of the lesson that, while economic assistance had been difficult to translate into durable political influence, military aid alone was also an inadequate instrument for this purpose. Consequently, the Soviet leader looked to political organization and ideology as the tools which might enable them to help their clients stand up more successfully to domestic opposition (i.e., which would make these revolutions, unlike their bourgeois predecessors, irreversible) and would bind these states to the Soviet Union so tightly that they could even maintain economic ties with the West (and therefore not become an economic burden on the Soviets) without jeopardizing the political, diplomatic and strategic relationship which was of utmost concern. In keeping with this conception, the Soviets pressed these allies to accept far more active Soviet involvement in regime-maintenance, without which foreign policy gains could not be consolidated.

In Ethiopia, for example, the ruling military Dergue, though already highly dependent on direct Soviet military assistance to prosecute the war against Eritrean and Tigrean secessionists, was nevertheless strongly urged to transform itself into a Marxist-Leninist Party (the Workers' Party of Ethiopia). The same thing had already happened in Mozambique, Angola, and South Yemen (PDRY). In all cases, Soviet advisers were actively involved in such matters as party organization, selection and training of personnel, and internal security (in which East Germans often played a major role). According to one observer, Soviet leaders in the late Brezhnev period viewed political organization and ideology "as among the most powerful of the tools available to them for furthering their realpolitik ends."[23]

Although such measures yielded successes in terms of entrenching Soviet influence, the successes themselves were increasingly resembling Pyrrhic victories by the end of the Brezhnev era, and skepticism was voiced more openly during the brief tenure of Yuri Andropov. For one thing, the objective of stabilizing the Soviet position through a combination of military assistance, political organization and ideology remained highly elusive. Most of these ideologically committed vanguard regimes faced protracted insurrections, as did the Soviet-backed Afghan communist government and the Sandinistas in Nicaragua. For another, the cost of keeping such regimes in power, not to speak of the larger cost of sustaining the entire Soviet overseas empire, placed a growing burden on a Soviet economy decreasingly able to bear such a burden. According to one study, the overall cost of empire — meaning implicit trade subsidies, export credits, military and economic aid (net of hard currency sales), incremental costs of "imperial" military operations (especially Afghanistan), and covert operations in developing countries — was estimated at $36-47 billion in 1980, as opposed to $14-22 billion in 1971 (in constant 1981 dollars). Of this, about $13-15 billion was directly attributed to the Third World, a figure roughly equivalent to 2 percent of Soviet gross national product.[24]

Perhaps most ironically, Soviet activism, rather than enticing additional forces to accommodate themselves to the wave of the future, actually provoked anti-Soviet fears and resentments around the world. It was sometimes said that the fulfillment of the Soviet wish for the triumph of communism in China, Afghanistan and Eastern Europe meant that the Soviet Union was the only country in the world surrounded by hostile communist neighbors. A similar byproduct of success was now evident in the Third World, where apparent Soviet gains in the superpower competition for influence and presence led to disenchantment with the

Soviet model of development, resentment and ingratitude by the recipients of Soviet support and assistance, and a growing tendency among domestic opponents of favored regimes and in nearby countries threatened by Soviet power to cooperate more closely with the West, especially the United States.

And in the United States itself, the vigorous assertion of Soviet power in the Third World led to a general hardening of public attitudes, reversing the neo-isolationism spawned by the Vietnam War. These changes thwarted any further improvement in bilateral Soviet-US relations and brought to power an American administration committed to a major military buildup and a confrontationist posture around the world. Given the rising costs and risks of Soviet activism and the questionable return on this investment, it is not really surprising that a major reassessment of Soviet involvement in the Third World was undertaken in the 1980s. What is striking is that it did not take place sooner.

Chapter 2. The Soviet Record in the Middle East

Nowhere are the dilemmas of Soviet Third World policy more vividly illustrated than in the Middle East. Indeed, the Middle East encapsulates the entire Soviet experience in the Third World, provides a template for the Soviet view of the issues at stake there, and constitutes the most meaningful test case for any Soviet reevaluation of established behavior in international affairs, that is, for new political thinking itself. The baseline for any such test, of course, is the Soviet record in the area before 1985.

Russian interest in the region long predates the Bolshevik Revolution. The historic outward thrust of the Russian heartland involved continuous absorption of Islamic territories in the Caucasus and central Asian regions and conflict with Islamic states. A central feature of the "Eastern Question" which vexed much of late nineteenth century diplomacy was Russian aggrandizement at the expense of the Ottoman Empire, accompanied by efforts to establish a cultural and political presence within Ottoman territory. Russia's southward expansion also brought it up against the Persian Empire and led to continuous friction with Great Britain over Afghanistan, in what the British called the "Great Game" for domination of the Indian subcontinent. Russia's longstanding aspiration to control the Turkish Straits was finally conceded by Britain and France in a secret diplomatic protocol during World War I, and might have been realized had not the Bolshevik Revolution intervened.

After the Revolution, however, the preoccupation with consolidating Soviet power and dealing with far more urgent concerns in Europe produced a policy of passivity verging on indifference for most of the inter-war period, the ideological justification for which has already been discussed. Cooperation with bourgeois or feudal nationalist regimes in Turkey, Iran and Afghanistan ostensibly served the purpose of frustrating imperialist (i.e., British) designs in that part of the world, but in effect it amounted to abandonment of communist and other revolutionary forces. The importance of a presence in more remote parts of the region was so slight that the Soviets voluntarily closed their diplomatic mission to Saudi Arabia in 1938.[1] It is true that the Molotov-Ribbentrop Agreement of 1939 stipulated that "the area south of Batum and Baku in the general direction of the Persian Gulf is recognized as the center of the aspirations of the Soviet Union," but this was almost certainly more a reflection of German hopes (or subtle warnings about interference in Eastern Europe) than of Soviet intentions.[2]

There were hints of a more activist policy immediately after World War II. The Soviets made abortive efforts to secure a trusteeship over Libya or at least to gain access to bases there and in the Dodecanese Islands. The issue of the Straits was again raised in the form of a demand to revise the Montreux Convention governing their use, and the Soviets also demanded the return of the northeastern Turkish towns of Kars and Ardahan which they had ceded to Turkey after World War I, but both demands were rebuffed. The Soviets were slow to evacuate troops stationed in northern Iran and conspired to set up a puppet regime in Iranian Azerbaijan, but a combination of Iranian political finesse and western diplomatic pressure eventually produced a Soviet withdrawal and the collapse of the "autonomous" State of Azerbaijan. In the early post-war years, Stalin's interest in the Middle East was therefore confined to his own immediate periphery — especially Turkey and Iran — and even there, he was unwilling or unable to push very hard to secure the control or predominant influence to which he undoubtedly aspired, relying, instead, on the rather unpromising instruments of propaganda and local communists. These Soviet probes undeniably contributed to the emergence of the Cold War environment; American containment policy, in general, and the Truman Doctrine, in particular, stemmed directly from perceived Soviet challenges in this so-called "northern tier" (and its westernmost extension, Greece). But although Stalin pushed, the effort he invested, the risks he was prepared to assume, and the alacrity with which he retreated when faced with the threat of resistance all reflected the low priority assigned this area in Soviet policy. And further afield in the Middle East, he refrained from any efforts at all to intrude into areas of acknowledged western primacy, so much so that he once rejected a request from King Farouk for arms to drive the British out of Egypt, arguing (according to Khrushchev) that the Near East was part of Britain's sphere of influence and that the Soviet Union "couldn't go sticking our nose into Egypt's affairs."[3]

Not until Khrushchev began to exploit the potential opportunities presented by local nationalism did the Soviet Union leap over the periphery and inject itself into the heartland of the Middle East. Even then, Soviet activism was as much a function of security considerations as a manifestation of ideological reformation. American containment policy rested in large measure on the deterrent power of US forces, deployed around the world in the political framework of regional treaty organizations. Technological limitations in the early part of the Cold War dictated the siting of bombers, and later of intermediate-range ballistic missiles, in bases surrounding the Soviet Union, including some in the Middle East. The incorporation of the "northern tier" countries — Turkey, Iraq, Iran, and Pakistan — in the Baghdad Pact virtually closed the geographical gap between NATO and SEATO and made manifest the traditional Soviet fear of "capitalist encirclement."

Soviet concerns with western influence in the Middle East, and particularly with its military dimensions, coincided with those of the republican government in Egypt. Intensely proud, suspicious of the British (and all their allies), and resentful of Iraq's challenge to Egypt's self-ascribed preeminence in the Arab world, Gamal Abd al-Nasir had sufficient reasons of his own to oppose the Baghdad Pact. Despite their initial misgivings about the bourgeois-nationalist character of the regime, the Soviets therefore agreed in 1955 to provide Egypt with arms, thus vaulting over the "northern tier" and breaking the western monopoly on military relationships in the heartland of the Middle East. The fact that this first transaction was given a Czech cover suggests that the Soviets were somewhat apprehensive about the audacity of the move, but western responses simply created opportunities for the further consolidation of Soviet-Egyptian relations. In Abd al-Nasir, the Soviets found a dynamic leader wedded to the brand of anti-western neutralism characteristic of the post-Bandung era in the Third World.

After the nationalization of the Suez Canal and the political victory he scored over Britain and France in 1956, Abd al-Nasir's regional and international stature soared and he became an immensely effective practitioner of "objectively anti-imperialist" policies. His aggressive promotion of "Arab socialism" and "Arab unity" threatened traditional regimes throughout the Middle East as well as the western interests — bases, communications, oil, and the political relationship underlying all these — that they served. Despite their encouragement of the generally "progressive" trends in Egyptian domestic policies during this period and their readiness to award certificates of ideological approval, the Soviets did not delude themselves that Abd al-Nasir's regime was moving toward scientific socialism; as Khrushchev candidly admitted, "I am a communist and he is the leader of the Arab national liberation movement. He does not share our political views. But when we exchanged opinions on the situation which had arisen in the Middle East there was mutual understanding — I understood him and he understood me."[4] But this was not the Soviets' primary concern. Indeed, they did not even evince much interest in the fate of Egyptian communists persecuted and imprisoned by the Egyptian authorities. What mattered most was that the regime be encouraged and assisted to continue undermining western interests in the area and to provide a secure base for the political battles of the Cold War. And in this sense, the strategy appeared to be working throughout most of the 1950s and 1960s.

During this period, decolonization and domestic upheavals brought to power a number of regimes eager to distance themselves from the West and accept Soviet assistance, along with the presence and influence that went with it. In North Africa, independent Morocco and Tunisia were ruled by nationalist regimes intent on maintaining close ties with the West, though willing to establish normal diplomatic and commercial relations with the Soviet Union. But in Algeria, the triumph of the national liberation movement brought to power a radical government committed to an interpretation of non-alignment that resulted in growing economic and military reliance on the Soviet Union. By a similar process, the independence of South Yemen in 1969 led to the replacement of British control by a pervasive Soviet presence.

Aside from decolonization, the Soviet position in the region benefited from the radicalization of domestic politics there. The 1958 military coup in Iraq overthre a traditional pro-western regime and established the Soviet Union as the foremost great power patron in that country; military coups in the late 1960s produced the same outcome in Libya and the Sudan. Even regimes willing and able to resist closer links with the Soviet Union were susceptible to influences which favored Soviet aims in the region. Nationalist pressures prevented Jordan from joining the Baghdad Pact and necessitated the elimination of a direct British role in the Jordanian army. The royalist regime in Yemen signed a Treaty of Friendship and Cooperation in 1956 and concluded an arms deal with the Soviet Union in 1957, as did the Syrian government in 1956, *before* military coups in those countries brought to power regimes with the ideological attributes normally characteristic of Soviet allies or clients.[5] Only Iran and the Arabian Peninsula (apart from the Yemens) appeared immune to Soviet inroads, although even Iran began a limited military supply relationship with the Soviet Union in 1967 and Kuwait did the same in 1977.

In short, the exploitation of anti-western nationalism permitted the Soviet Union to expand dramatically its political and military presence in the Middle East. Starting from a negligible base in the mid-1950s, it had, by the early 1970s, become the predominant foreign power in Egypt, Syria, Iraq, Algeria, Libya, Sudan, and the Yemens. It had gained base rights or access to naval and air facilities in several countries and broken the western military monopoly in the Mediterranean. And it developed a huge market for Soviet arms which, especially after the mid-1970s, became a lucrative enterprise and a major source of Soviet hard currency revenues. The extent to which this area figured in Soviet arms exports is illustrated by the fact that of the $83 billion in weapons actually delivered to non-communist Third World countries between 1956 and 1985, the Middle East and North Africa consistently took over 70 percent; only in the period 1981-85 did the share fall below that, and then only to 68 percent.[6] But within the region, arms transfers were even more concentrated on countries which could pay hard currency (or have it paid for them). From the mid-1970s to the mid-1980s, Iraq, Syria and Libya probably accounted for three-quarters or more of total regional deliveries, and in the period 1979-83 these two, along with Algeria and India, took over 70 percent of the global total of approximately $40 billion.[7]

Even in purely economic terms, however, the picture was not one of unqualified gain. The initial drive for a Soviet presence in the region involved a substantial economic cost. Not only were arms offered on highly favorable terms; the Soviets provided assistance for economic development programs, particularly showcase projects associated with modernization and industrialization. The Soviet decision to build the Aswan Dam in 1956 was as politically significant as the "Czech" arms deal of the year before. From 1954 until 1985, the Soviet Union agreed to provide almost $33 billion in economic assistance and actually delivered over $15.6 billion. Of this, almost half consistently went to Middle Eastern and North African clients (except during the period 1975-79, when the share rose to over 75 percent).[8] During the first decade-and-a-half, the value of economic commitments actually exceeded that of military transfer agreements, although the fulfillment rate of military agreements was greater. However, the growth rate of military sales was consistently higher and the increasingly commercial basis of arms transfers during the second half of this 30-year period, and especially since the mid-1970s, meant that during the late 1970s and early 1980s there was little or no net economic cost for Soviet involvement in the region as a whole, and there may even have been a net benefit.[9]

On the other hand, the more concessionary policies of the earlier period meant that some countries still had large outstanding debts which might never be recovered. Egypt, for example, had accumulated a military debt of $3 billion by the mid-1970s and Syria, despite the increasing emphasis on cash sales, owed the Soviet Union as much as $20 billion by the late 1980s.[10] Moreover, there were large but incalculable indirect economic costs. A semi-captive market for Soviet industrial exports, for example, may have disguised inefficiencies and artificially prolonged the viability of outdated production techniques, thereby postponing needed reforms and doing long-term damage to the domestic economy and international competitiveness of the Soviet Union.

On balance, however, economic benefit was not the primary motivation for Soviet engagement in the Middle East (or elsewhere in the Third World). Soviet leaders sometimes indicated that they expected an economic return from their investment, even at the outset of their involvement in the area. Khrushchev, for example, writes at one point that he approached the Aswan Dam decision as a profitable business transaction: "We had to make sure that the Egyptians could repay us in regular deliveries of their best long-fiber cotton, rice, and other goods."[11] Of course, disinterested altruism was always stressed as a reason for Soviet support, but in general the purpose was to advance the cause of anti-imperialism, that is, to promote Soviet political, security and ideological objectives, and it is in that larger context that the costs and benefits and risks and opportunities must be viewed.

However, the balance even in these terms was also increasingly ambiguous. The greatest Soviet strategic successes were registered precisely at a time when their intrinsic value was being challenged by technological changes, especially the development of secure, second-strike nuclear arsenals built around land- or sea-based systems with intercontinental range. In these circumstances, the importance of overseas bases and facilities for national security was far less obvious than it had been during the early post-World War II period, not to speak of the Victorian Age before World War I.[12] If force deployments and access agreements in the Third World contributed to Soviet security in the 1970s and 1980s, it was more in the sense of ideological affirmation than of the ability to defend the Soviet state against the major threats.

Moreover, the deepening involvement of the Soviet Union in the region subjected it to a variety of serious costs and risks. One of the major advantages that the Soviet Union initially brought to the Middle East — beyond the northern tier — was a reputation unsullied by acquisitive habits of its own or association with other imperialist powers. Indeed, the Soviets could credibly present themselves as proven opponents (and victims) of the same imperialist powers so hated by Arab and even Iranian nationalists. This advantage, however, was a wasting asset. After the dissolution of the western colonial empires, protectorates, and preferential treaties guaranteeing military or economic concessions, the interests of the Soviet and local partners began to diverge. Middle Eastern regimes focused more on domestic or regional objectives, whereas the Soviet Union still concerned itself primarily with imperialism, albeit of a different type: the global presence of the United States. In this competition, the comparative advantage of the Soviet Union was not so apparent. Indeed, as their position seemed to improve in the formal sense described above — more countries on the map listed in the Soviet "column" — the Soviets increasingly became victims of their own successes.

At one level, this was simply because familiarity breeds contempt. The closer the economic and military relations between the Soviet Union and various countries in the region, the more the shortcomings of Soviet industrial products and economic assistance came to be appreciated. The more intrusive the presence of Soviet advisers and instructors, the more resentment they tended to arouse, particularly when they showed ignorance of or contempt for local sensitivities. The massive Soviet military advisory mission sent to Egypt after the Six-Day War in 1967 provoked considerable animosity, especially among senior Egyptian military officers, because of the arrogant and condescending attitudes of many of its members. According to President Sadat, one reason for his decision to expel the Soviet mission in 1972 was that "the Soviet Union had begun to feel that it enjoyed a privileged position in Egypt — so much so that the Soviet ambassador had assumed a position comparable to that of the British High Commissioner in the days of British occupation of Egypt."[13] Even in the best of circumstances, such human frictions were probably unavoidable, but when advisers were seen as the embodiment of Soviet support for an unpopular regime, they themselves became the target of opposition elements. In 1980, Muslim Brotherhood resistance to the government of Hafiz al-Asad in Syria included attacks on Soviet personnel, two of whom were killed in Hama.[14]

The most serious problems, however, were intrinsic, structural tensions stemming from the divergent perspectives of a superpower patron and almost any local client in an international system essentially defined by superpower rivalry. At the risk of oversimplification, transactions between superpowers and Third World regimes resembled market relations in which the commodity is power: the superpowers sell or lend it, and local regimes buy or borrow it.[15] Third World actors need this power because they cannot generate enough of their own to secure or maintain their rule and pursue their policy objectives. This need creates the demand for supplementary power of one sort or another. The supply is explained by the superpower desire for the currency of exchange in this transaction — influence. As long as the primary objective of Third World actors coincided with that of the Soviet Union — the elimination of direct imperial control of the Middle East — it was sufficient for the Soviet Union to assist them to promote this objective, i.e., to achieve what one observer has termed "complementary influence."[16] But when this objective had largely been accomplished, the local actors turned to domestic or regional objectives, which usually meant the prosecution of domestic or regional conflicts, whereas the Soviet Union aspired to a more active or coercive influence, involving at least some kind of economic, cultural and/or military presence, and ideally the ability to enlist local regime support for broader, global objectives. In this marketplace where power was traded for influence, superpowers were competing for the alignment, allegiance and sympathy of Third World regimes, a kind of twentieth century equivalent of historical rivalries for overseas empires.

The global scope of the Soviet-American rivalry made the market a zero-sum game; the basic threat to one superpower (and the basic opportunity for the other) was the defection or overthrow of an allied regime. To avoid the first outcome, superpower patrons had to avoid alienating local allies. In practice, this limited the superpowers' ability to prevent local allies from using the power they had bought or borrowed in pursuit of their own domestic or regional objectives, even if those objectives did not necessarily coincide with those of the superpower. Indeed a superpower, once engaged, found it difficult to deny requests for even more power. Superpowers were rarely willing to restrain determined allies from acting in ways that provoked or exacerbated conflicts. Instead, they often found themselves supporting these allies when they were threatened by domestic or regional adversaries, regardless of how or why the allies got into trouble.[17] Since commitments once assumed had to be honored, local allies learned that in most cases they could independently pursue their own agendas, secure in the knowledge that they "will be protected whatever happens."[18]

All of this suggests a central paradox of patron-client relations in a bipolar system: influence can be retained only if it is not exercised. If presence, economic assistance, military aid, and even ideological affinity do not produce durable influence, then the conceptual basis of superpower involvement in the Third World becomes highly dubious. Rather than promoting durable achievements in the global balance, it leads to essentially formal gains, themselves often ephemeral, which involve high costs and high risks. This is particularly so if the allied regimes are weak and vulnerable to their domestic or regional opponents, which was frequently so in the case of Soviet allies. As a result, the Soviets repeatedly encountered the following types of dilemmas in the Middle East:

1. the defection of seemingly secure allies to the rival superpower;
2. entrapment in protracted, inconclusive domestic conflicts;
3. commitments to local clients in conflict with one another, leading to difficult choices and the alienation of one, if not more of those clients;
4. commitments to local allies in conflicts with local allies of the United States, which prevented progress in bilateral relations and sometimes led to superpower crises involving a choice between loss of position and the risk of a direct clash with the United States.

All of these dilemmas stemmed from the basic problem for the Soviet Union following its initial gains: commitment without control. Over the course of time, its clients used, bought or borrowed power to pursue policies that brought them into conflict with domestic or regional rivals, and then pressed the Soviet Union to provide continuing support, to the point where such support jeopardized other Soviet objectives in the region or elsewhere in the international system.

Client Defection

The most dramatic instance of client defection was the case of Egypt under Sadat. The earliest and greatest Soviet investment in the Third World had been made in Egypt. Since the initial breakthrough in 1955, the Soviets had provided huge amounts of economic and military assistance, and, after 1967, direct military support in the form of advisers, technicians, and ultimately even combat forces. During the 1973 war, they undertook a massive airlift to resupply Egyptian forces. Throughout this period, they had consistently provided strong diplomatic support for Egypt's positions in a variety of issues, and particularly in its conflict with Israel.

In return, they had acquired impressive levers of ostensible influence and a direct payoff in terms of global strategic deployments. Thousands of Egyptian military personnel had been trained in the Soviet Union, and the massive presence after 1967 gave Soviet advisers direct access, not only to the military establishment down to the battalion level, but also to the intelligence services and the ruling Arab Socialist Union. In the context of the military deployment in Egypt in the late 1960s and early 1970s, the Soviets were given exclusive jurisdiction over three Egyptian airfields — Inshas, Jiyanaklis, and Mansura — and were also operating their own aircraft out of three others, Cairo, Aswan, and Beni Suweif.[19] They also had regular use of port facilities in Alexandria and Port Said. As a result, the Soviet Union acquired some of the power projection capabilities commensurate with the status of a global superpower which it had consistently sought.

In short, Egypt was the focus of the greatest effort in Soviet Middle East policy; indeed, it was the largest single recipient of Soviet assistance in the Third World. Of all noncommunist countries, it was the one with the largest Soviet presence and the one in whose domestic political system the Soviets were presumably best able to operate. And it was the one in which the Soviet Union had acquired the most visible and important strategic assets. But despite this intricate web of relations, Egyptian President Sadat demonstrated that, short of large-scale military intervention with all its risks and costs, there was little the Soviet

Union could ultimately do to prevent a determined local ally from acting independently of Soviet preferences and ultimately turning his back on the Soviet patron and realigning his country with the United States. Of course, the reorientation was neither simple nor abrupt. Instead, it was played out over a period of at least two years, beginning with the expulsion of the Soviet advisers in July 1972. Even then, Egypt continued to receive sophisticated Soviet weaponry, and it was only in 1974 that the partnership with the United States fully developed and relations with the Soviet Union seriously deteriorated, culminating in the break in diplomatic ties in 1976.[20] Moreover, the essential precondition for all this was the fundamental redefinition of Egyptian objectives with respect to the conflict with Israel. Nevertheless, the magnitude and gravity of the shift made it a major setback in and of itself, and it exposed with brutal clarity the fact that any return on the Soviet investment in the Middle East, however great, was inherently tentative and transitory.

Quagmires

The desire to preserve established positions not only meant a constant Soviet concern with the possibility of defection by allied regimes; it occasionally also led to active Soviet intervention to protect seemingly loyal but incompetent allies from their own domestic opponents. Indeed, this motive appears to explain in large part the major military commitments of the Soviet Union during the 1970s: in Angola and, on the fringes of the Middle East, in Ethiopia and, most massively, Afghanistan.

Until April 1978, Afghanistan was a feudal-bourgeois, nonaligned but cooperative Soviet neighbor — a kind of underdeveloped Finland.[21] In that month, a military coup brought to power the People's Democratic Party, a Marxist-Leninist vanguard party committed to the forced-pace transformation of Afghanistan into a socialist society, bypassing the capitalist stage of development. Soon after taking office, the PDP began to implement such measures as the redistribution of land, the cancellation of debts, the repression of Islamic institutions and dignitaries, limitations on forced marriage and bride-price, and the introduction of compulsory political-education classes under the guise of an anti-illiteracy campaign. These measures provoked serious tribal and religious resistance, especially after the more radical Khalq faction of the party, led by Nur Muhammad Taraki and Hafizullah Amin, ousted its Parcham rivals in early 1979. By the middle of the year, widespread defections from the Afghan Army and rebel attacks had resulted in the loss of several provincial capitals and the deaths of hundreds of Soviet military advisers.

Apart from one report that a local KGB officer promised the communist conspirators Soviet support for their proposed coup nine days before it took place, there is no direct evidence that the Soviet Union was involved in or even aware of the coup that brought the PDP to power.[22] The previous government, which had kept Afghanistan quiet, friendly, and in the Soviet "sphere of influence," presented no real challenge to Soviet interests. But the new leadership, which had longstanding ties with the Soviet Union, promised to turn Afghanistan into a progressive, quasi-Marxist state even more firmly in the Soviet orbit. Soviet decision-makers, used to viewing the world through an ideological prism, could only interpret the political change as an important gain. The problem was that this Afghan government suffered simultaneously from infantile leftism, administrative incompetence and military impotence. It had provoked a revolt which it was unwilling to appease and unable to repress. And if it were overthrown by its domestic opponents, post-revolution Afghanistan might well be more pro-American or pro-Chinese than the pre-revolution regime had ever been.

Moreover, the Soviets found it difficult for ideological reasons to refuse requests for ever-more economic, technical and military assistance; as one analyst put it, the USSR "has never met a self-professed, pro-Soviet Marxist-Leninist group to which it would not extend assistance, either to seize power or remain in power."[23] Thus, when the PDP purged the government of all civil servants of questionable loyalty, there were not enough qualified Afghans left to run the bureaucracy and hundreds of Soviet civilian technicians were brought in to fill the gap. And when purges decimated the officer corps and defections cut troop strength by half, Soviet arms transfers and the advisory mission were substantially augmented.

Despite this assistance, PDP policies continued to alienate the population and the resistance gathered strength. In March 1979, the rebels temporarily overran Herat in western Afghanistan and dozens of Soviet advisers were killed, some after being publicly tortured. Soviet dependents were then withdrawn from the country and military assistance was stepped up again, but there was no sign of either a willingness to moderate government policies or an ability to contain the rebellion. By the summer of 1979, the Soviets were clearly concerned about the very survival of the regime, and to prevent its collapse they ultimately resorted to massive military intervention at the end of December.

This was not their initial inclination. Before the actual invasion, Soviet emissaries had twice tried to organize a coup against Hafizullah Amin (who had eliminated Taraki in September) and KGB advisers had tried to take over the Afghan secret police. There were also reports of three attempts to assassinate Amin and even of a Soviet offer to the Afghan Islamic League to abandon the PDP leadership and set up a "government of national unity." Only when all these measures proved abortive did the Soviets decide on direct, large-scale military intervention.

If their previous reluctance reflected Soviet fear of being dragged into an Afghan quagmire, these fears were clearly borne out by what happened afterward. Soviet troop strength in Afghanistan quickly reached 110-120,000 and remained at that level for over eight years of indecisive warfare. Soviet casualties continued to mount, there were persistent reports of demoralization in the field and resentment at home, and the material cost of the occupation was estimated at about $16 billion during the first five years; from 1982 to 1985 alone, the Soviet Union delivered over $2.5 billion in weapons to the Afghan armed forces.[24] But heavy pressure on the Soviet-installed leader, Babrak Karmal, to moderate his domestic policies did not result in any weakening of the resistance. More importantly, the Soviet military intervention in Afghanistan, undertaken to rescue a Marxist-Leninist regime from its own folly and weakness, alienated a large number of other Third World countries, particularly in the Islamic world, and accelerated a hardening of American public opinion, leading to a major American military buildup and a more confrontationist foreign policy during the 1980s. In short, Soviet commitment without control in Afghanistan produced dubious local gains which entailed very high direct costs and major setbacks to larger Soviet interests.

The High-Wire Balancing Act

The difficulty of managing such commitments also emerged in a variety of conflict situations involving more than one Soviet client or protege. When conflicts broke out between regional actors already aligned with the Soviet Union or which the Soviet Union wanted to cultivate, Soviet leaders were forced to make difficult, sometimes impossible choices. Support for one side alienated the other; neutrality tended to alienate both. The natural inclination of the Soviets was to try to resolve these conflicts in a way that preserved good relations with both sides, ideally by refocusing their attention on the issue which had originally facilitated their entry into the region — imperialism (and/or its Israeli manifestation, Zionism). In the Arab heartland of the Middle East this was sometimes successful, although even then Soviet diplomatic agility was not sufficient to prevent temporary threats or setbacks.

In 1958, for example, the pro-British Hashemite regime in Iraq was overthrown by a group of military officers led by Brigadier Abd al-Karim Qasim. Qasim quickly took Iraq out of the Baghdad Pact, reoriented Iraqi foreign policy toward the Soviet Union, proclaimed his dedication to Arab unity, and instituted a domestic policy of radical reform. Nevertheless, before the end of the year, Qasim was engaged in a vicious struggle with Abd al-Nasir, ostensibly over the terms and conditions of Arab unity, and for almost five years Egypt and Iraq fought a war of unrestrained propaganda attacks and mutual subversion. The Soviets, eager to retain good relations with both sides, tried to mitigate the intensity of this struggle by urging Abd al-Nasir to moderate his attacks, but the chasm was so great that they were eventually forced to choose. The fear of a revived western presence in Iraq if

Qasim fell, combined with his alliance with local communists, led the Soviets to support Iraq, and the result was a distinct chill in Soviet-Egyptian relations and a brief Egyptian flirtation with the United States, in which context the United States resumed economic aid to Egypt (including $150 million a year in surplus food). In this case, the problem of straddling two stools was eased when Qasim was overthrown in 1963 and Egyptian-Iraqi enmity diminished.[25]

A similar dilemma arose on several occasions in the 1970s and 1980s because of conflicts between two other favored Middle Eastern clients, Syria and the Palestine Liberation Organization (PLO). As in the case of the Egyptian-Iraqi rift, the Soviet Union was embarrassed by the need to choose (though it normally came down on the Syrian side), but it was able to avoid truly serious, long-term damage to its position.

In the Horn of Africa, however, the outcome was far worse.[26] The Soviet Union had had an arms supply relationship with Somalia since 1963 and relationships were intensified after 1969, when a military junta led by Muhammad Siad Barre took power and committed Somalia to the path of "scientific socialism." The intimacy of Soviet-Somali ties was symbolized by the 1974 Treaty of Friendship and Cooperation, the vehicle for Soviet access to naval and air bases in Berbera and Mogadishu. For Somalia, the most emotive policy issue was the reunification of Somali people in the Horn, but as long as Somali irredentism targeted western-controlled or -aligned states such as Djibouti, Kenya, and Ethiopia, Somali aspirations did not contradict broader Soviet purposes. However, the collapse of Ethiopian Emperor Haile Selassie's regime in 1974 and the progressive radicalization of the Dergue government which succeeded it immensely complicated the issue from the Soviet point of view. The Dergue's radicalism and repressive domestic policies, and particularly its violation of human rights, led to a rapid deterioration in US-Ethiopian relations and strengthened the inclination of some of its members to establish links with the Soviet Union. The first manifestation of this initiative was a military supply agreement in December 1976; in February 1977 the US Military Advisory Group was expelled and US access to a huge communications facility was cut off. Soviet leaders had every reason to view Ethiopia's realignment as a net gain in their competition with the United States, but it placed serious strains on the Soviet-Somali alliance, since Somali leaders had an altogether different foreign policy agenda.

The Soviet Union, of course, was not eager to jeopardize old gains for the sake of new ones. In the early part of 1977, Soviet diplomacy therefore tried to obfuscate the Somali-Ethiopia contradiction by supporting Cuban leader Fidel Castro's proposal that both countries join South Yemen in a Red Sea "progressive front" aimed at frustrating the plans of the United States and its conservative Arab allies. Somalia, however, cared more about its regional aspirations than about Soviet global concerns; for the Somali leadership, it was more important to exploit the chaos in Ethiopia than to preserve Soviet goodwill (especially since the "American option" appeared increasingly feasible). Siad Barre therefore continued to support Somali rebels in the Ogaden — the Western Somali Liberation Front — and in mid-July regular Somali forces were committed in strength to the war.

Even after the invasion, the Soviets tried to maintain good relations with Somalia; in August a new Soviet-Somali economic assistance agreement was signed. Nevertheless, the large-scale intervention of Cuban troops and Soviet advisers to help stem the invasion was more "even-handedness" than Siad Barre could tolerate. In November, he announced the expulsion of all Soviet advisers from Somalia, the withdrawal of all base rights, the renunciation of the Soviet-Somali treaty, and the breaking of diplomatic relations with Cuba. In early 1978 the Ethiopian-Cuban-Soviet counter-offensive broke the back of Somali forces in the Ogaden and forced Siad Barre to withdraw from Ethiopia, thereby consolidating the Soviet position in that country, but the price was virtually complete reconciliation between the United States and Somalia. By the end of 1979 agreement in principle had been reached on a package of US military and economic assistance in return for access to the former Soviet bases in Berbera and Mogadishu. A bilateral agreement in August 1980 formalized this arrangement.

Whether or not this realignment constituted a net gain for the Soviet Union is difficult to judge; precise measuring instruments for such a calculation do not exist. What is clear, however, is that the Soviet government could not force actual or desired allies in the Third World to subordinate their own concerns to broader Soviet global objectives, and within the framework of those objectives any gain involved some cost. In this case, the Soviet government was itself forced to make a painful choice between Ethiopian and Somali nationalism, and its choice consolidated the Ethiopian gain (at least temporarily), but at the cost of alienating the Somali side.

In other cases, the Soviet Union was better able to manage a delicate balancing act and avoided the complete alienation of either side. Even in those cases, however, the price was considerable resentment on both sides, so that Soviet successes had a tentative and fragile character. The most prominent example of such a dilemma in the Middle East was the Iran-Iraq War.

The outbreak of that war in 1980 again involved a high-intensity, high-stakes conflict between two local powers, one of them an important Soviet ally for many years, the other a formerly pro-western state whose revolutionary government was now exceedingly hostile to the United States.[27] In the mid-1970s, Iraq had been perhaps the closet Soviet ally in the Middle East (with the possible exception of South Yemen). Following the 1972 Treaty of Friendship and Cooperation, Soviet arms and advisers flowed into Iraq and notwithstanding the tremendous increase in Iraqi oil revenues during the second half of the decade, the Soviets even provided about $150 million in economic assistance.[28] Despite growing Iraqi economic and military trade with the West, some significant differences on regional issues, and domestic repression of Iraqi communists, Iraq remained an important focus of Soviet activity in the Middle East and the Soviet Union remained Iraq's largest supplier of military assistance. At the same time, the Islamic revolution in Iran was a tremendous setback to the American position in the area and created possible opportunities for Soviet presence or influence which the Soviets were eager to exploit. This objective was pursued by "undermining the moderates within the revolution, supporting the extremist clerics, exacerbating the hostage crisis, and raising the specter of an American military threat."[29] To justify this approach, Soviet analysts performed ideological contortions, arguing, for example, that the attitude toward Islamic fundamentalism depended on its content and the "state of class forces."[30] In Iran itself, the Communist Party (Tudeh) also supported Khomeini unreservedly and applauded the most radical elements in the Islamic Republican Party, a posture undoubtedly intended to ensure the survival of Tudeh as the only organized secular force in the event that the Islamic regime collapsed. It was even alleged that in the early fall of 1980, the Soviets warned Iran of an impending Iraqi attack and offered to supply arms and internal security assistance.[31]

The Iraqi invasion greatly complicated the Soviet desire to maintain or cultivate good relations with both sides, since it could not demonstratively support one without risking the alienation of the other. Moreover, the war jeopardized broader Soviet designs in the region. At a minimum, it diverted attention from the Arab-Israel conflict, from which the Soviets could extract far more political advantage because their positions conformed with the general preferences of the entire Arab world. And with the Arab world itself split over the Iran-Iraq War, any Soviet move which could be interpreted as partiality might alienate Arab supporters of one or the other of the belligerents. Finally, prolonged fighting, with its attendant risks of collateral damage to pro-western regimes, oil installations and transportation networks, might provoke large-scale American military intervention in the region.

This complex of considerations led to a posture of official neutrality coupled with frequent appeals for an end to a war from which only the United States and Israel could benefit.[32] In material terms, the Soviets tried to manage a finely-tuned assistance program which responded to the needs and requests of both sides without providing either with a war-winning capacity or causing the irrevocable alienation of either. Following the invasion, with Iran on the defensive, the Soviets refused Iraqi requests for new deliveries, but they fulfilled existing contracts for small arms, ammunition and spare parts. Meanwhile, Soviet proxies or allies — Eastern European states, North Korea, Libya and Syria — became major suppliers of Iran. In mid-1982, Gulf Cooperation Council foreign ministers claimed that Soviet, East German and Cuban experts were present in Iran and a western source estimated the number of Soviet military advisers alone at 1500.[33] When the tide of war seemed to shift in the middle of 1982, the Soviets resumed the shipment of major weapons systems to Iraq, and both military and economic assistance were stepped up in the following years. However, they also sought to improve bilateral relations with Iran, primarily through economic means, while supporting the actions of other allies to enhance Iranian military capabilities.

This difficult balancing act produced occasional setbacks of a serious nature. Even after the resumption of major arms sales to Iraq in mid-1982, President Saddam Hussein still complained that the Soviet-Iraqi Treaty had not worked.[34] He continued the Iraqi reorientation toward the West (and toward pro-western states in the Middle East), culminating in the resumption of US-Iraqi diplomatic relations in 1984. However, the tilt toward Iran had not produced any concrete gain in the form of a pro-Soviet regime or meaningful Soviet influence there. Instead, the Islamic Republic continued to denounce the Soviet Union as the "little Satan" and remained vociferously critical of Soviet policy in Afghanistan. In early 1983, Iranian authorities outlawed the Tudeh Party, accusing it of sabotage, espionage and infiltration of the army and Revolutionary Guard on behalf of the Soviet Union, at the same time expelling 18 Soviet diplomats for having interfered in Iran's internal affairs by "establishing contacts and taking advantage of treacherous and mercenary agents." And when new Soviet weapons (especially surface-to-surface missiles) were later used to inflict heavy civilian casualties on Iran, the regime's suspicion of Soviet motives was compounded by intense popular hostility.

By the mid-1980s, the Soviet Union had managed, at some considerable material cost, to maintain tenuous links with both Iran and Iraq, but it was not able to convert those links into serious influence, and its position in both countries was fragile. Once again, the prism through which the Soviet Union viewed its role in the Third World made it hostage to the demands of those local actors whom it wished to cultivate. In the case of the Iran-Iraq War, the contradictory requirements of local actors in conflict with each other had not inflicted excessive risks and costs on the Soviet Union, but they had produced the embarrassment of a policy which seemed increasingly pointless and aimless.

The Linkage Problem

The last type of dilemma in which the Soviet Union often found itself, involved conflicts between its own clients or allies and those of the United States. These potentially offered the greatest benefit but also implied the greatest risk, because if one of the belligerents got into serious trouble, its superpower patron would be confronted with a cruel choice: abandon a protege to its fate, meaning an immediate loss of position and a tarnished reputation for credibility elsewhere, or else intervene to preserve a local asset, meaning a risk of confrontation with the other superpower. In the latter event, objectives at the bilateral superpower level, such as arms control agreements or improved economic relations, would be jeopardized even if a military crisis were averted. Since the Soviet Union often found itself aligned with the weaker protagonist in regional conflicts, the burden of intervening more often fell on it, but since the Soviets suffered from inferiority in both the central strategic balance and in force-projection capabilities for much of the period under review, and since they developed a progressively greater interest in bilateral detente, they found this burden increasingly onerous and costly. Moreover, the costs and risks inherent in this dilemma were increasingly borne for the sake of holding operations; there are very few instances in which a "milieu" gain for the Soviet Union, meaning an improvement in the Soviet-American balance of influence due to a change of regime or regime-orientation, can be directly attributed to Soviet support for allies in regional conflicts.

There are numerous examples of violent regional conflicts with a more or less pronounced "East-West" coloration to them: the Algerian-Moroccan border clashes in the early 1960s and their later conflict over the Western Sahara; Libya's confrontations with most of its neighbors, especially Egypt in the late 1970s and Chad in the 1980s; the Yemen War of the later 1960s and South Yemeni tensions with Oman and North Yemen in the 1980s; the Syrian invasion of Jordan in 1970 and Syrian-Jordanian border tensions in 1980; and others. But in terms of the structure of Soviet-American competition, none of these conflicts was a case of "high-interest symmetry" because the Soviet Union, though more closely identified with one of the protagonists, had a substantive interest (whether out of local or regional considerations) in limiting the damage to its relations with the other protagonist, an interest which went beyond the avoidance of a superpower crisis.[35]

The Middle East regional conflict in which these countervailing considerations least obtained was the Arab-Israel conflict, and it is therefore not surprising that this conflict held out the greatest opportunities, elicited the greatest Soviet investments in and commitments to one side, and provoked the gravest Soviet-American crises in the Third World.

The advantage of Soviet support for the Arab cause against Israel was two-fold. First, it played on an emotional theme that resonated across the entire Arab world (though with varying degrees of intensity). It could therefore be invoked to complicate the formation of any "pro-western" bloc in the Middle East and to obscure inter-Arab differences that confronted the Soviet Union with uncomfortable choices. Secondly, it enabled the Soviets to contrast their own position with American equivocation on the issue, thereby locating their allies in the region on the "moral high ground" while forcing "pro-American" regimes into a defensive posture. Indeed, the desire to tar the United States with the brush of guilt by association and to exploit Arab hostility to Israel for anti-American purposes explains the dominant motifs in Soviet public analysis and diplomacy for close to three decades: the equation of imperialism and Zionism, and the congruence between the Soviet-American conflict and the Arab-Israel conflict. Even late into the Brezhnev era, this tendency was reflected in the writings of those who would subsequently be portrayed as prominent "new thinkers." In 1979, for example, Yevgeny Primakov, a leading Soviet authority on the Middle East (and winner of the Nasser Prize), wrote that the USSR "supports the Arab national-liberation movement and Arab peoples which are the targets of Israel's expansionist policy; the USA backs Israel's rulers, who are pursuing an overall Middle Eastern policy coordinated with world imperialism." Since the conflict was not between two nationalisms, but rather between imperialism and the national-liberation movement, there was really no choice at all for the Soviet Union; its position was predetermined by proletarian internationalism.[36] In short, the Soviet Union, given its conceptual approach to the Third World, preferred the polarization of the Arab-Israel conflict along lines parallel to the Soviet-American conflict.

All of these changes appear to reflect a revolution in Third World policy under Gorbachev, meaning a major shift in priorities within the Third World and an all-embracing devaluation of the Third World as a factor in Soviet foreign policy. The ideological element in Soviet calculations has undoubtedly diminished, and the willingness to pressure local allies or deny them resources, even at the risk of losing them completely, has correspondingly grown. Nevertheless, neither the discontinuities with the pre-1985 record nor the consistencies since then should be exaggerated.

The intellectual origins of new political thinking can be traced back into the late Brezhnev era, at least insofar as disillusionment with the so-called revolutionary democracies and vanguard parties is concerned.[36] In the late 1970s, economic ties with these forces became less imbued with a political thrust as skepticism grew about the political utility of Third World radicalism. As a result, foreign economic relations were placed on a more pragmatic, less generous and "altruistic" basis. The onerous needs of Cuba, Mongolia and Vietnam made the Soviet Union extremely reluctant to take on additional obligations to other "states of socialist orientation." One result was that Mozambique's application to join the Council for Mutual Economic Assistance (Comecon) was rejected in 1981.[37] The emphasis on mutually beneficial ties with more advanced, capitalist Third World states intensified during the brief tenure of Yuri Andropov, who was said to be particularly skeptical about the "revolutionary-democratic" school of thought in Soviet foreign policy.[38] Moreover, the preference for predictable relations with capitalist-bourgeois partners is not necessarily evidence of a non-competitive world view or of new political thinking in the more comprehensive sense associated with Gorbachev; Khrushchev and Lenin also cultivated ties with non-Marxist albeit anti-imperialist forces, but they clearly aimed at weakening the West (and were more optimistic about a subsequent transition to socialism than their successors in the 1970s and 1980s could possibly be). However, this was not the only practical manifestation of embryonic new political thinking before Gorbachev; even under Konstantin Chernenko, an old-line Brezhnev functionary, the Soviet Union would not provide decisive backing to radical clients in Mozambique and Angola and left them no option but to sign agreements with South Africa in 1984 (the Nkomati and Lusaka Accords, respectively) which obliged them to restrain two other Soviet proteges — the African National Congress and SWAPO.[39]

This objective dictated virtually complete identification with and backing for the Arab cause against Israel, the only consistent qualification being a Soviet refusal to endorse any calls for Israel's destruction.[37] Soviet public diplomacy provided unswerving support for Arab positions in the United Nations and other international forums, significant economic assistance and massive arms transfers, and, in particularly critical circumstances, the threat of or even the recourse to direct military intervention. This was accompanied by a campaign of domestic propaganda which took on even shriller tones after the spontaneous Soviet decision to sever diplomatic relations with Israel in 1967. For a long time thereafter, the distinction between political indoctrination and officially-endorsed anti-Semitism was blurred in analyses such as the one which appeared in *Komsomolskaya Pravda* on October 4: "The Zionist big Jewish bourgeoisie in various countries is endeavoring to suppress the struggle of the broad toiling masses for their freedom and independence.... The ideologists and leaders of Zionism are only flunkies at the beck and call of a rich master whose nationality is exploitation and whose god is the dollar."[38]

But if the desire to secure or preserve Arab alignment with the Soviet Union dictated support for Arab allies in their conflict with Israel, broader global concerns — especially the desire (indeed, the absolute imperative) to avoid a direct clash with the United States — implied avoiding situations in which the Soviet Union would be called upon to intervene directly in military hostilities. These two requirements formed the outer parameters of Soviet policy on the Arab-Israel conflict, and they often left Soviet leaders with uncomfortably little room to maneuver.

Soviet leaders were under no illusion that the nexus of their relationship with the most important Arab allies was anything other than military; Khrushchev freely acknowledged that "we were cautious toward people who adopted the word Socialism but who seemed mostly interested in getting military aid from us."[39] The Soviets were particularly aware of the dangers of direct involvement. In January 1970, at the height of the Egyptian-Israeli War of Attrition, the ineffectiveness of Egyptian air defenses forced Abd al-Nasir to request Soviet crews to operate aircraft and anti-aircraft missiles. Brezhnev's response was that this would be a step with serious international implications and had all the makings of a crisis between the Soviet Union and the United States. "We are the strongest power on earth," Brezhnev told Abd al-Nasir. "But you must understand that this will involve a considerable risk, and I don't know that we are justified in taking it."[40] But when Abd al-Nasir replied that he would return to Egypt and tell his people "that the time has come for me to step down and hand over to a pro-American President" the Soviets overcame their reservations and complied with the request.

This was not the first time that the Soviets tried to avoid crisis-producing actions of their own or to persuade their allies to do likewise. The entire history of Egyptian-Soviet relations between 1967 and 1972 (retold with great bitterness by Sadat in his autobiography) essentially involves a Soviet effort to restrain Egypt from going to war and to withhold the support and equipment — especially deep-strike aircraft — that would make that possible. And when war nevertheless broke out, the Soviets strongly pressed Sadat to accept an early ceasefire, presumably because they feared (prematurely, but not wrongly) that Israel would turn the tide and impose difficult and costly choices on the Soviet leadership.[41] Long before that, in a rather different context, Khrushchev had made it clear to Abd al-Nasir that Soviet maneuvers in the Transcaucasus might help dissuade western intervention in Iraq following the military coup of 1958, but that the Egyptians should not misinterpret this move as a willingness to move any closer to a confrontation.[42] Out of the same desire to forestall regional developments that could lead to crisis, the Soviets also urged their Syrian allies to refrain from invading Jordan in 1970 and Lebanon in 1976. In the latter case, expressions of Soviet displeasure included withdrawal of advisers from Syrian units entering Lebanon and the temporary manipulation of the flow of arms.[43]

In all these cases, Soviet and local ally priorities clearly diverged; in none of them were the Soviets unwilling to press their own priorities to the point where that would jeopardize relations with the Arab ally. In other words, the competitive dimension of Soviet involvement in the region — the compulsion to preserve (and if possible enhance) the balance of "influence" with the United States — normally took precedence over any inclination to restrain local allies. The commitment to the Arab cause which flowed from that motivation had two decisive consequences. The first was that it denied Soviet diplomacy the flexibility that might have contributed to a political settlement of the conflict. The zero-sum perspective enabled Arab allies to exploit the Soviets for their own purposes (just as it often allowed "pro-western" Arab states like Kuwait or Jordan to manipulate the United States by playing "the Soviet card"). During the intensive negotiations with the United States following the Six-Day War, for example, the Soviets signaled a clear desire to collaborate and in private discussions showed a readiness to distance themselves from maximal Arab positions. Nevertheless, Ambassador Anatoly Dobrynin made it clear to his American interlocutors that the Soviets "would not separate themselves from Egypt, and if Nasir would not accept the American proposals, neither would the Soviet Union."[44]

The second result was that the Soviets found themselves obliged to come to the active assistance of Arab allies in desperate situations, despite their attempts to dissuade the very same allies from a course which produced these situations and despite their own awareness of the risks. The 1970 intervention in the Suez Canal Zone has already been discussed. However, the most notable, and dangerous example of such a rescue operation was the Soviet threat to intervene against Israel following the breakdown of the Egyptian-Israeli ceasefire on October 22, 1973, and the nuclear alert and superpower crisis which ensued. It may be argued, of course, that it was really the threat of American intervention on behalf of Egypt which convinced Israel to stop fighting and later to open a supply route to the trapped Third

Army, thereby diverting events from what appeared to be a collision course. But in addition to any expectation of creating a more manipulable Egyptian-Israeli environment for negotiations, the American action was almost certainly intended to forestall the need for Soviet intervention to save Egypt, thus averting the danger of a superpower confrontation. In this sense, at least, the Soviet threat achieved its stated objective. In 1956 and 1967, Soviet threats against Israel, though less credible, less dangerous, and virtually unconnected with Israeli decisions to stop fighting, nevertheless also added at least an incipient atmosphere of superpower crisis to the regional conflict dimension.

It should not be inferred from the above that Soviet policy was exclusively passive or reactive. The same competitive analytical framework that usually led the Soviets to acquiesce in Arab demands whatever their own reservations also prompted them to take initiatives that exacerbated existing conflicts, subverted conflict resolution processes, and even provoked armed hostilities. The 1973 War, for example, was launched contrary to Soviet preferences, but once it did break out, the Soviets incited Iraq and Algeria to join in.[45] On at least two occasions, the Soviets opposed and tried to subvert processes that held out hope for peaceful settlements of the Arab-Israel conflict but appeared to enjoy American support, hence, to serve American interests. In the first case — the Camp David Agreements of 1978 — the Soviets were simply conforming with the preferences of important Arab allies (especially Syria) and had no countervailing interest in the Arab party to that process; Egypt, by then, was already firmly in "the American camp." But in the second case — the 1985 Hussein-Arafat Agreement — apprehension about American gains (coupled, to be sure, with attention to Syrian preferences) sufficed to produce Soviet opposition to a plan which even one of its own local partners — the PLO — had endorsed.

The most noteworthy example of Soviet destabilization was the incitement of Egypt, particularly the false warnings of Israeli troop concentrations on the Syrian front, which eventually culminated in the 1967 war.[46] In Abd al-Nasir's mind, the fact that this "information" had been volunteered by the Soviets could only be interpreted as a Soviet invitation "to stir up the question of

Israeli-Arab military relations with their implicit support."[47] Of course, an argument can be made that even this initiative was "reactive" in the context of threatening regional and international trends: Egypt's inconclusive and debilitating war in Yemen; the domestic fragility and military vulnerability of the radical "left-Ba'th" regime in Syria (in April, the Israel Air Force had shot down six Syrian aircraft over Syrian territory); the emergence of an anti-Nasir Islamic bloc led by Saudi Arabia; and negative developments in the global "correlation of forces" — the overthrow of Soviet Third World proteges such as Sukarno, Nkrumah, and Ben Bella, and even the recent military coup in Greece. Heightened Arab tensions with Israel, though not a war, might at least provide temporary relief from these problems and help reinforce the position of Abd al-Nasir and, by extension, the Soviet Union. But even if one assumes that Soviet behavior was motivated by need rather than opportunity, the perception of need was itself a function of the role ascribed to the Middle East (and the Third World in general) in the Soviet competition with the United States. It was the determination to prosecute this competition that led to Soviet policies that were costly, sometimes dangerous, and often futile; whether or not these policies were active or reactive, provocative or defensive, was of lesser consequence.

As Khrushchev's aforementioned complaint about socialist allies demonstrates, Soviet leaders were aware that their efforts to exploit regional conflicts for the sake of their global aspirations often resulted in the exploitation of their global conflict for the sake of allies' regional aspirations. As Brezhnev's unenthusiastic response to Abd al-Nasir's pleas in 1970 demonstrates, Soviet leaders were acutely aware of the dangers and risks of their Middle Eastern posture, especially on the Israel-Arab conflict. There is considerable indirect evidence that both the strategy and the tactics of this posture came under occasional criticism. Khrushchev, for example, in defending his own record regarding Egypt, makes a cryptic reference to "those narrow-minded skunks who raised such a stink and tried to poison the waters of our relations with Egypt."[48] And following the 1967 War, there were rumors of serious recriminations within higher Party circles, including one to the effect that the Secretary of the Moscow City Soviet had been deposed after objecting to any further support for the Arabs.[49] But whatever the frequency or intensity of the criticism, it did not repudiate the zero-sum view of relations with the United States in the Third World or discredit the fundamental premises of Soviet involvement in the Middle East — particularly, that political, economic and military support for anti-western regimes yielded returns worth having in terms of Soviet standing as a global power. Consequently, commitments to local allies normally continued to prevail over all other considerations.

Despite occasional precursors of new political thinking, it was not until Gorbachev that the underlying premises of policy were themselves subjected to serious and far-reaching reassessment.

Chapter 3. New Political Thinking and the Third World

Although the Soviet Union under Brezhnev never explicitly renounced the principle of "peaceful coexistence," neither did it ever argue or act as though peaceful coexistence was inconsistent with intense East-West competition, including a struggle for influence and presence in the Third World. Shortly after taking power in 1964, Brezhnev stressed the objectives of "supporting liberating revolutionary movements" and "comprehensive development of solidarity and cooperation with the independent states of Asia, Africa and Latin America." In 1971, the 24th CPSU Congress instructed the Central Committee to "extend and strengthen the ties with the revolutionary democratic parties of the developing countries...in the interest of the common struggle against imperialism."[1] By contrast, the 27th Congress in 1986 (the first under Gorbachev) made scant reference to the Third World and virtually ignored the Arab-Israel conflict. Indeed, Gorbachev's was the first report of a general secretary since Georgi Malenkov's in 1952 not to address itself explicitly to the problems of the Third World.[2]

This contrast symbolizes the major transformation in Soviet attitudes toward the Third World. The transformation, of course, is hardly confined to the issue of the Third World alone. In fact, changing Soviet views of the Third World are derivative of changing views on far more fundamental questions: the Soviet relationship with the United States and Soviet security doctrine, the link between foreign and defense policies and the domestic system, and ultimately the character of the Soviet political system, Soviet society, and the Soviet state itself.

In the late 1960s, the Soviet Union entered a lengthy period of continuous stagnation and, by the late 1970s, actual decline. By one estimate, the average annual growth rate of Soviet GNP fell from 5.3% in the 1966-70 Plan Period to 3.7% in 1971-75 and 2.7% in 1976-80. At the same time, factor productivity per composite unit of labor and capital increased by 1.1% in 1966-70 but was actually negative in the following two periods: -0.5% in 1971-75 and -0.8% in 1976-80.[3] A prominent Soviet economist portrays a slightly less gloomy picture, claiming that national income grew by 41% during 1966-70, 28% in 1971-75, 21% in 1976- 80, and 16.5% in 1981-85, but admits that these figures overstate real growth rates because they ignore foreign trade balances (which were deteriorating over time) and rely on artificially low price indices which understate the effect of inflation.[4]

Furthermore, much of the growth that did take place was concentrated in the heavy industry and defense sectors, meaning that deterioration in the social sphere was more pronounced than general economic performance figures would indicate. Soviet citizens suffered from a growing housing shortage, declining delivery of health services, environmental damage on a monumental scale, and consumer goods (including food) of shoddy quality, when they were available at all. In short, the quality of life in the Soviet Union was deteriorating in almost every respect, and it was no consolation that life expectancy, contrary to the trend in every other industrialized country, was also declining.[5]

All of this amounted to what one Soviet analyst has called the "crisis of the Stalinist and neo-Stalinist social system."[6] The basic cause of that crisis was gross inefficiency in the utilization of resources, itself due to the command economy, administration by injunction, and the attempts by central planners in Gosplan to direct the entire economy of the country on the basis of quantitative targets. The Soviet economy, of course, had suffered from these inefficiencies and the distortions they encouraged from the earliest days of collectivization. The history of Soviet economic management is one of wastefulness, sloth, corruption and falsification of statistics in order to conceal failures to fulfill and overfulfill arbitrary production and procurement quotas.

But as long as the motor of the economy was extensive growth, i.e., the massive application of new resources — land, labor and capital — at the margins, it was possible to tolerate such inefficiencies and still achieve growth. Given the seemingly inexhaustible resource base of the Soviet Union, even the fact that these resources were expropriated by administrative edict was not, whatever the cost in human suffering, incompatible with economic growth. During the ninth five-year period (1971-75), however, even the Soviet Union ran into serious resource constraints. The growth rate of the major production inputs — manpower, fuel and raw materials, capital investments, and industrial assets — began to slow down, and it continued to diminish thereafter until the mid-1980s.[7] As a result, any new economic growth could only be intensive, that is, it required far greater efficiencies than the old system permitted. Indeed, it is no accident that the single most authoritative definition of perestroika focuses precisely on this concept. "Perestroika," wrote Gorbachev, "is the all-round intensification of the Soviet economy...."[8]

Intensification, in turn, depends on higher factor productivity, especially labor productivity. The initial inclination was to achieve this through top-down reform, by emphasizing order, discipline, better organization and responsibility. Thus, Gorbachev's short-term solution to stagnation was to attack corruption and the Soviet work-ethic. Initial measures included a concerted drive on drunkenness, which was responsible for much absenteeism and defective production in Soviet factories. It quickly became clear, however, that a real change required incentives other than moral exhortation ("Fulfill the Plan"), repression (threats of dismissal, if not worse) or deprivation (of vodka). Higher worker productivity depended on the promise of more and better consumer goods, and this meant a shift in priorities away from heavy industry and military production. Higher productivity from capital depended on the modernization of the obsolete production base (plant and equipment) and of industrial and agricultural organization, as well as on advanced science and technology, which could not be adopted and applied without a freer flow of information, not just within the country but also across national boundaries. And activating the human factor depended on a broader change in the moral and psychological situation of the country, i.e., on a real shakeup of the economic and political systems to ensure greater responsiveness and accountability of the leadership, what Gorbachev calls "a broad democratization of all aspects of society."[9] In short, eliminating the "braking mechanism" — the command system — responsible for economic stagnation necessitated profound changes across the entire spectrum of Soviet life.

Politics aside (and we have seen that "hard-soft" or "right-left" oscillations in domestic and foreign policy often coincided), structural factors made it impossible to confine these reforms to internal matters alone. For while the most blatant manifestations of the crisis were domestic, the crisis had a serious external dimension, as well. Despite the apparent advances of the 1970s, the Soviet Union was looking less and less like a true superpower. Apart from military strength, it had none of the accouterments of superpower status: economic power, advanced technology, dependable allies, or an attractive cultural, political or developmental model. The Soviet Union which Gorbachev inherited stood in marked contrast to Khrushchev's Soviet Union, which could boast of impressive economic reconstruction, scientific achievements (symbolized by Sputnik), and the admiration of national-liberation movements and newly-independent countries, or even to Stalin's Soviet Union, which (despite the enormous human costs) projected a viable model of rapid modernization and industrialization and inspired strong communist movements in Europe.[10]

Gorbachev himself stressed the organic tie between domestic and foreign policies, arguing that "we need lasting peace in order to concentrate on the development of our society and to cope with the tasks of improving the life of the Soviet people."[11] In fact, a restructuring of the Soviet economy required more stable and predictable relations with the West, especially the United States, for at least three reasons: first, to avoid increasingly burdensome arms races and permit the diversion of increasingly scarce resources to civilian investment and production (conversion); secondly, to facilitate the participation of the Soviet Union in the international division of labor, i.e., in those economic institutions, such as the General Agreement on Tariffs and Trade, which could stimulate economic growth; and third, to break down the political barriers to western capital (in the form of credit or direct investment in joint ventures) and technology (the flow of which was constrained by Cold War mechanisms such as COCOM).

Pursuing these objectives implied a fundamental reappraisal of Soviet security doctrine and foreign policy, the result of which is termed "new political thinking" (see Appendix). In the security sphere, reductions in military expenditures would stem from (or be rationalized by) the acknowledgement that the traditional reliance on unilateral measures to maximize military capabilities did not provide real security anyway. Given that security was indivisible and arms races were futile, the old approach needed to be replaced by comprehensive, multilateral measures, including arms control agreements aimed at eliminating overall imbalances and specific asymmetries. The need to escape from the arms race trap became particularly urgent in the mid-1980s because the potential catalyst of a major new spiral in defense expenditures — the American Strategic Defense Initiative — was taking shape just when the Soviet economy was least able to sustain the massive cost of responding to such a challenge. Indeed, the anticipated cost of matching American buildups was so great that even if mutual restraint through arms control remained elusive, the necessary reduction in the Soviet defense burden might in any event be achieved by determining force levels on the basis of "reasonable sufficiency" and reconfiguring remaining forces for "non-aggressive [or "defensive] defense."[12]

More generally, the conceptual underpinnings of Soviet foreign policy since the Revolution came under serious challenge. The class basis of international politics was downplayed in favor of the primacy of law and of "universal human concerns." "General interdependence," wrote Gorbachev, means that "it is essential to rise above ideological differences." If only because of nuclear weapons, the conflict between the two social systems must not lead to world war, and all crises must therefore be settled by peaceful means, on the basis of "balance of interests" rather than "balance of power."[13]

The principles of new thinking which ostensibly inspire Soviet foreign policy in the era of perestroika cannot rigidly constrain Soviet behavior or provide specific guidance for action; most of them are cast at a very high level of generality which permits flexible interpretation in accordance with circumstances. Many of them are not even new. Gorbachev was certainly not the first Soviet leader to appreciate the awesome destructiveness of nuclear weapons, and the overall objective of *detente* guided policy with respect to the United States during much of the Brezhnev era (and for many of the same reasons). Indeed, the impetus for domestic reform and "peaceful coexistence" can be traced at least to the 20th Party Congress of 1956; Gorbachev explicitly acknowledges his intellectual debt to Khurshchev and regrets that the latter's effort to improve the international situation "came up against a brick wall of incomprehension and resistance."[14]

Two things are new, however. The first is the forthright admission that the Soviets have no monopoly on truth. By accepting the diversity of the world rather than insisting on the universal validity of scientific laws of socio-economic development, Gorbachev effectively justifies the "deideologization" of Soviet foreign policy, thereby eliminating at least the doctrinal basis of the "two-camps" approach to international politics.[15] Since the redefinition of security as mutual or interdependent simultaneously undermines the geostrategic basis for this world view, the logical result is abandonment of "zero-sum thinking" and an emphasis on the cooperative rather than the competitive dimension of US-Soviet relations.

The second innovation is the recognition that the improved East-West relationship on which economic restructuring depends is itself highly dependent on Soviet behavior in the Third World. In other words, new political thinking accepts the inevitability of the "linkage" that old political thinking denied and rejected for so long. Writing in 1981, a prominent Soviet academician ridiculed not only the validity of "linkage," but even its very possibility. Denying that it had ever engaged in destabilizing behavior, he conceded only that the Soviet Union might have a disruptive impact because of "the force of its example as a country which freed itself, in 1917, from neocolonialist exploitation by foreign capital, nationalized foreign property, and achieved impressive economic progress without outside aid."[16] But seven years later, a widely-cited article by Vyacheslav Dashichev admitted: "We were wrong in assessing the global situation.... Though we were politically, militarily (via weapons supplies and advisers), and diplomatically involved in regional conflicts, we disregarded their influence on the relaxation of tension between the USSR and the West...."[17]

Pushed to its logical limit, this reassessment would culminate in Soviet disengagement from the Third World, especially in the military sphere. After all, such involvement in Third World affairs was an economic liability, produced geostrategic gains of highly dubious relevance to national security as perceived in new political thinking, and constituted, at best, an irritant to US-Soviet relations, hence to the domestic objectives of perestroika, and, at worse, a source of direct superpower confrontation, hence a potential threat to survival. These themes have been repeatedly echoed in the increasingly open debate about the Soviet role in the Third World. For example, an unsigned editorial article in *International Affairs*, a journal with close ties to the Foreign Ministry, argued that glasnost should be extended to the question of Soviet economic and military assistance to Third World countries, because "our involvement in their affairs is a substantial burden on our economy and may also have a considerable impact on the international situation in general and our standing in the world in particular. We need to restore a truthful picture of what is going on in the Third World that has been distorted by looking at it through ideological spectacles."[18] Nothing could better reflect the revolution in the analysis of the Third World than this criticism; in the not too distant past, it would have been heretical to suggest, at least in public, that the truth could be understood in any way other than "through ideological spectacles."

Moreover, the analytical case for retrenchment coincided with growing popular resentment at Soviet support for Third World causes and with the conviction (sometimes buttressed by racist stereotypes) that Third World parasites were responsible for Soviet economic stagnation. In more elegant terms, commentators would claim that improving domestic living standards was far more important for national security "than the course developments may take in some exotic country that many of us can barely find on the map of the world."[19] Such sentiments pointed to embryonic isolationism, a kind of "Russia First" school of thought in foreign affairs which some analysts began to discern in the 1980s.[20] However, this orientation was still only "a marginal tendency in Soviet Third World policy, given the near-consensus within the policy elite for maintaining the Soviet role as a competitive global power."[21] "Proletarian internationalism" may have been discarded as a basis of Soviet policy, but even considerations of prestige dictated that there would be no wholesale liquidation of Third World assets.

Consequently, the Soviets began to implement what one observer has called a "synthesis" intended to permit continued involvement in the Third World at lower risk and cost while removing it as a major obstacle in the Soviet-American agenda.[22] This involved two shifts in emphasis. The first was the "demilitarization" of policy, by playing down the conflictual dimension and instead promoting the political resolution of disputes. The second — justified by the principle of universalization of foreign relations — was the increased attention to more stable, prosperous, capitalist Third World states at the expense of ties with radical, anti-American, left-wing but dependent vanguard revolutions or regimes.[23]

The most dramatic example of "demilitarization," of course, was the Soviet withdrawal from Afghanistan, which was completed on schedule in February 1989. This was often hailed by the Soviets as an example of how disputes could be settled by peaceful means and international cooperation. In fact, Afghanistan was in many respects sui generis, since it was the only case of massive, direct Soviet military involvement, and that dimension of the conflict could be "resolved" by unilateral action. Despite Soviet efforts to promote negotiations (including direct talks with various Afghan rebel groups in late 1988 and early 1989), there was no resolution of the conflict in Afghanistan and hostilities continued long after the Soviet withdrawal.

Nevertheless, the decision to withdraw without a political settlement ensuring the survival of the client regime implied renunciation of the traditional practice of "chasing petty and essentially formal gains associated with leadership coups in certain developing countries."[24] And that reasoning led the Soviet Union to encourage allies and clients to negotiate compromise settlements of other regional conflicts, even at some risk to allied interests, hence, to its own position.

Thus, in Southern Africa, the Soviet Union began to push the MPLA government in Angola to negotiate with western-backed

UNITA rebels and was an important broker of the December 1988 agreement which led to the withdrawal of Cuban troops from Angola and the independence of Namibia; in 1989, it also announced the withdrawal of Soviet military advisers from Mozambique.[25] In the Horn of Africa, it attempted to resolve regional and domestic conflicts by renewing ties with Somalia in 1986 and pressing the Marxist government of Ethiopia to negotiate a settlement with Eritrean and Tigrean rebels; the latter effort met with little success — instead, the government continued to fight until it was overthrown in 1991 — but the seriousness of Soviet intentions was reflected in a willingness to strain ties with the Dergue, to the point where Mengistu was told by Gorbachev not to expect any more military aid after 1990.[26] In East Asia, "demilitarization" of Soviet policy was reflected in the withdrawal of Soviet troops from Mongolia, support for the withdrawal of Vietnamese forces from Cambodia in September 1989, and the pullout of most Soviet forces from Vietnam.[27] And in Latin America, the Soviet Union pressed the Sandinista regime to begin negotiations with the contra rebels in late 1987, reduced military assistance in 1989, and encouraged the Sandinistas to accept the free elections which resulted in their ouster from power in February 1990.[28]

As the Soviets tried to cut back their economic, military, and political commitments to revolutionary but generally backward clients, they made a determined effort to cultivate relations with more prosperous and promising economic partners in the Third World. The intention to undertake such a reorientation was signaled early on at the 1986 Party Congress, which declared Soviet "sympathy" for the "liberated countries" rather than "international duty" toward them, and indicated that "states of socialist orientation" should expect Soviet support only "to the extent of its ability."[29] The rationale was stated most baldly by Foreign Minister Edward Shevardnadze, who declared, "We must enhance the profitability of our foreign policy and achieve a situation in which our mutual relations with other states burden our economy to the least possible extent...."[30]

For the same reason, the Soviet Union counseled its allies against a hasty and premature transition to socialism and encouraged them to maintain or expand their economic ties with the

West. In the mid-1960s, Khrushchev had preached the virtues of collectivized agriculture to Abd al-Nasir; in the late 1980s, Soviet advisers were lecturing to the Vietnamese about the advantages of opening up to the world market and warning the African National Congress against excessive nationalization of private property.[31] Meanwhile, the Soviets themselves were working hard to expand relations with western-aligned, capitalist states, including some which it had previously spurned either on ideological grounds or in deference to the policies of their regional partners. The most prominent example of this was the progressive improvement of links with South Korea, beginning with the Soviet decision not to boycott the 1988 Olympic Games in Seoul, including the establishment of a South Korean trade mission in Moscow and the discussions of joint ventures in 1989, and culminating in the meeting between Gorbachev and South Korean President Roe Tae Woo in San Francisco in June 1990.[32] But while South Korea was particularly attractive because of its potential ability to help in the development of Siberia, other possible sources of capital, technology, raw materials, or consumer goods were also cultivated at the highest level: Brazil, Argentina, and Mexico in Latin America, Zaire in Africa, and Thailand and Indonesia in Southeast Asia.

These specific examples of changes in regional emphasis took place within the framework of a declared doctrinal preference for greater political cooperation within the framework of international institutions, especially the United Nations, coupled with military and economic retrenchment abroad. The adoption of "multilateralism" is symbolized by the Soviet decision, in mid-1988, to pay long-overdue financial obligations for UN peacekeeping operations, and by Gorbachev's proposal, at the end of that year, for a much-expanded role for the UN in conflict prevention and international security. Retrenchment in the declarative sense is exemplified by Deputy Foreign Minister Vladimir Petrovsky's announcement in late 1989 that Soviet troops deployed abroad numbered 627,500 and that the objective was to have them all back in the Soviet Union by the year 2000.[33] Retrenchment in an operational sense is demonstrated, though far more ambiguously, by trends in Soviet arms transfers. The estimated value of agreements with the Third World (in constant US dollars) has dropped every year since

1984 (with the exception of 1987), and actual deliveries in 1986-89 were lower than in 1982-85 for most categories of weapons, in some cases significantly so.[34] A large part of this drop can undoubtedly be attributed to the decline in effective demand caused by the end of the Iran-Iraq War and diminishing revenues of oil exporting states; most other arms suppliers experienced similar declines in sales. In some cases, however, it also stems from a growing Soviet reluctance to pay the price (i.e., to provide credit or grant aid) for the political influence which arms transfers presumably bring, and even the United States Defense Department predicts that this reluctance will intensify in the future.[35]

On the other hand, there were sufficient examples of continuing Soviet support, including military support for enlisted allies to suggest real inconsistencies between the logic of new political thinking and the behavior of the Soviet government after Gorbachev took power. Despite year-to-year fluctuations, for example, there was no drastic reduction in the number of Soviet military advisers and technicians in Third World countries; in 1990, they numbered about 16,100, below the level of the mid-1980s but still almost as high as the 1981 figure of 16,750.[40] Furthermore, Soviet forces did assist local allies to escalate hostilities. Offensives in Afghanistan increased markedly for two years after Gorbachev took power, and various forms of military pressures were applied against Pakistan, as well.[41] Soviet advisers and Cuban forces spearheaded Angolan government offensives in 1987 and 1988, even after negotiations had begun.[42] Arms transfers to most "progressive" regimes were maintained and even stepped up, often on easy terms or as outright grants. Cuba, for example, received $6.15 billion in weapons during 1986-89, as opposed to $5.33 billion in 1982-85, and deliveries to Afghanistan rose from $2.51 billion to $9.08 billion, with a particularly large transfer of $3.8 billion in 1989, after the withdrawal of Soviet troops.[43] The willingness to make such a large financial commitment to the Afghan regime, despite the fact that physical backing had been withdrawn and at a time when the Soviet economy itself was on the verge of disintegrating, suggests that there might have been some unique factor at work in this case, perhaps connected to the nationality problem within the Soviet Union itself. However, large amounts of aid were also being provided in the late 1980s to other traditional recipients. Despite a 20 percent reduction in Soviet-bloc military aid, Nicaragua still received $300-500 million in financial assistance in 1989. Moscow continued to subsidize Cuba at the rate of about $6.5 billion per annum (including $1.5 billion in military assistance), mainly through the sale of oil at below-market rates and the purchase of sugar at above-market rates. However, there were reports of a perceptible drop in assistance in 1990 and consequently, of serious economic hardship in Cuba itself.[44] Angola got about $1-1.5 billion in 1989, direct military assistance to Ethiopia totaled $800 million-$1 billion, and aid to Cambodia was doubled to $500 million.[45]

There are a number of possible explanations for the apparent failure to implement fully the principles of new political thinking in the Third World. One of these has to do with bureaucratic politics. In principle, the top Soviet leadership should have more freedom to innovate in foreign and defense policy, especially on a relatively marginal matter such as Third World policy, than it would have to revolutionize domestic structures. In home affairs, thorough-going political and economic reforms jeopardize the power and vested interests of a huge nomenklatura and challenge the Soviet social contract based on job security and assured access to basic goods and social services at subsidized prices in exchange for a low standard of living and political quiescence.[46] Nevertheless, certain institutional interests do act to constrain flexibility in foreign policy as well. It has been suggested, for example, that during Andrei Grechko's tenure as minister of defense in the 1970s, "the military had been a major enthusiast for Third World involvement and later reportedly favored the intervention in Afghanistan."[47] Another observer attributes Soviet activism to a broader coalition, arguing that Brezhnev "had to defer to the wishes of a Third World policy working group composed of Ponomarev's ID [International Department], the Military, and the Main Political Administration."[48]

To the extent that these group interests (ideological or bureaucratic) played some role, it is not surprising that the ideas endorsed by Gorbachev but expounded primarily by civilian intellectuals could not be fully implemented until Gorbachev asserted his primacy over the conservative ideologues and interest group representatives. This did not really happen in the Party until Yegor Ligachev was shunted aside and the retirement of old-line Comintern ideologue Boris Ponomarev and his like-minded deputy Rostislav Ulyanovsky allowed Gorbachev to promote new thinkers in the International Department and/or to subordinate it to the Presidential Council and even to the Foreign Ministry, where concerns about relations with the United States were more highly developed. Indeed, it was only in September of 1989 that Gorbachev was able to remove two other formidable hardliners — former KGB head Viktor Chebrikov (an early Gorbachev ally) and Vladimir Shcherbitsky (the most veteran of Brezhnev's old cronies) — from the Politburo.[49] In the military, whose missions, budgets, and privileges would inevitably be jeopardized by any retrenchment, Gorbachev could not ignore powerful military lobbyists like former Chief-of-Staff Ogarkov or the pre-Gorbachev holdovers, including Defense Minister Sokolov and other reputed "interventionists" like Navy Commander Admiral Gorshkov and MPA Chief Yepishev. Only when the prestige and status of the military were reduced, and especially when the Mattias Rust affair of May 1987 provided the pretext for Gorbachev to appoint his own men as defense minister (Dimitri Yazov) and chief-of-staff (first, Marshal Sergei Akhromeyev, and later the relatively junior and obscure General Mikhail Moiseyev), could the military no longer be considered a truly formidable obstacle to retrenchment in the Third World.[50]

But however important institutional resistance may have been, it is not a sufficient explanation. After all, bureaucratic politics (especially those of the military) had never been decisive, given the armed forces' ultimate subordination to, and penetration by, the Party. Moreover, many inconsistencies persisted even after Gorbachev got fuller (though never absolute) control over the machinery of government. It is therefore likely that other factors also played a role, including conceptual confusion, perhaps combined with some measure of inattentiveness, at the very highest levels.

Perestroika and new political thinking did not spring full-blown from the mind of Gorbachev in March 1985. In an index of his published speeches and writings up to mid-1985, there was no entry for glasnost, nor did Gorbachev make any reference to democratization and plurality of opinions in the opening months of his rule.[51] Nothing hinted at his intention to elevate the government and an elected parliament at the expense of the Party or to curb the military (whose budget continued to grow at least until 1988). And there was nothing to suggest an impulse on his part to preside over the liquidation of the Soviet Empire — not the informal branch in the Third World and certainly not the more institutionalized branch in Eastern Europe.

Instead, the original point of departure appears to have been little more than a determination to rationalize and revitalize the economy. A set of general principles concerning the political, security and foreign policy corollaries of that objective could be formulated fairly easily and quickly thereafter because many of them — given their vague and innocuous character — had already been espoused in one form or another by previous leaders. Gorbachev's invocation of Lenin's teachings was utterly predictable, but his acknowledgement of an intellectual debt to Khrushchev's foreign policy was noteworthy, and has been mentioned. In domestic affairs he also credited the 20th Party Congress with major political, social and ideological measures, noting simply that these possibilities were not used to the full because of "the subjectivist methods adopted by the leadership under Khrushchev."[52] Still, the correct application of those principles was not always self-evident, and some measure of gradualism, incrementalism and learning by trial-and-error was probably inevitable. Moreover, following these principles to their logical conclusion led to operational decisions on specific issues which sometimes contradicted, not just the narrow interests of various constituencies, but the larger self-image of the Party and the state, and perhaps even the ethos of the Revolution itself. It would be perfectly understandable if even the top leadership should initially prefer to temporize and mitigate the negative consequences of such decisions, and to opt for reformism at the margins rather than revolution at the core.

Beyond the sheer force of inertia, that is, of changing the course of a heavy and ponderous state machine, overcoming inherent inhibitions required the sixth or seventh generation of an existing regime (as opposed to the first generation of a new regime) to mobilize all its determination and all its resources in order to repudiate its own past. Gorbachev and his collaborators found it extremely difficult to do this on issues such as the socialist economic system, internal Party organization, national security policy, nationalities, and center-periphery relations in the Soviet state, all of which were far more important and attracted a far greater share of their time, attention and political capital. It is therefore not surprising that Soviet policy on the Third World, despite the unquestionable impact of new political thinking, often proceeded on a hesitant, equivocal, and erratic course.

Chapter 4. New Political Thinking and the Middle East

For the Soviet Union, the Middle East is almost certainly the most important region in the Third World. It is the largest potential commercial market, the one to which large numbers of Soviet citizens feel the greatest cultural affinity, and — except for the socialist states (Cuba, Mongolia and Vietnam) — the one in which the Soviet Union has made the greatest commitments (including financial commitments which it would like to recover). And as the timeworn slogans about concern for developments in an area "adjacent to our southern borders" indicate, it is also the one in which perceived Soviet security interests are most directly at stake; as a diplomat involved in explaining Middle Eastern policy to Israelis and American Jews stressed, it is of utmost importance to ensure stability and tranquility in proximity to Soviet southern borders and to eliminate the foreign military presence "on our doorstep."[1] All these considerations would seem to portend sustained, and perhaps intensified Soviet engagement in the Middle East.

For the Soviet Union, the Middle East is also the most disruptive and dangerous region in the Third World. According to one veteran Soviet analyst of Middle Eastern affairs, the area has brought the world to the brink of nuclear catastrophe on four occasions: in 1956, 1967, 1973, and 1980.[2] Given the intensity of American interests and involvement and the need to improve relations with the West which flows from the preoccupation of perestroika with economic reform, these considerations would seem to indicate Soviet retrenchment and perhaps even disengagement from the Middle East.

These two contradictory impulses explain to a large degree why the inconsistencies and equivocations of Soviet Third World policy have found such prominent expression in the Middle East. In the broadest terms, Middle East policy has been informed by steady implementation of the principles of new political thinking: "demilitarization" and "de-ideologization" of Soviet involvement, more measured relations with radical forces coupled with a drive to diversify ties in the region (i.e., to cultivate important capitalist- and western-oriented countries), and an attempt to decouple Middle Eastern affairs from Soviet-American relations and promote the political resolution of conflicts, by encouraging local allies to moderate their policies and pursuing intensive consultations with the United States and all regional belligerents. However, this trend has not precluded frequent hints of ambivalence and even of reflexive reversion to "old thinking" along familiar East-West lines. And while the priority given to larger, global objectives has led the Soviets to risk greater friction with local allies than was generally the case before 1985, this did not mean that the Soviet Union was prepared to disengage completely from the Middle East and abandon all pretensions of superpower status.

Mikhail Gorbachev's accession to power did not produce any startling, immediate discontinuities in Soviet policy. Since the break with Egypt in the mid-1970s, Syria had been the most important Soviet ally and client in the Middle East, and one of Gorbachev's first high-level guests was President Hafiz al-Asad, who visited Moscow in June 1985. There was nothing in this visit to suggest that Soviet-Syrian ties or Soviet attitudes toward the Arab-Israel conflict were going to change. TASS reportage of the meeting repeated traditional propaganda themes, including denunciation of the "continuing aggressive actions of Israel with direct US support" and "the encroachments of imperialism and Zionism," and both leaders expressed their determination to strengthen the relations of friendship and trust between the two countries. Gorbachev and Asad also declared that a just and lasting peace could only be based on Israeli withdrawal from all occupied Arab territories and the establishment of an independent state for the Palestinians, to be pursued through an international conference and not through "separate deals with the aggressor," i.e., through direct negotiations.[3]

These themes were fully consistent with longstanding Soviet policies on the substance and procedure of Arab-Israeli peace, and they were taken almost verbatim from official pre-Gorbachev plans: Brezhnev's proposal of September 15, 1982 and Chernenko's of July 29, 1984, which differed only in that the former called for the attendance of all five permanent members of the Security Council while the latter recalled the precedent of the 1973 Geneva Conference and specifically mentioned only the United States and the Soviet Union. However the new leadership, especially after Edward Shevardnadze replaced Andrei Gromyko as foreign minister in July, signaled that the traditional guidelines of Soviet diplomacy on the Arab-Israel conflict were going to be challenged.

The first totem to be undermined was the virtual ban on direct, bilateral contacts with Israel. That barrier had never been absolute. Beginning with the Geneva Conference, Gromyko himself often met with Israeli foreign ministers at international gatherings, most recently with Yitzhak Shamir at the UN in 1984. But a secret meeting between the Israeli and Soviet ambassadors in Paris in July 1985 initiated a trend of increasingly frequent, open, high-level, institutionalized political contacts.[4] In August 1986, the first publicly announced talks were held by low-level officials in Helsinki, but the meeting, intended to clarify a Soviet request to send a consular team to Israel, broke off when Israeli representatives attempted to discuss Jewish emigration.

However, contacts between Israeli and Soviet advisers were maintained, and after a highly-publicized meeting between Prime Minister Shimon Peres and Soviet Foreign Minister Shevardnadze at the UN, the pace and depth of contacts picked up. In April 1987 Peres, by then vice prime minister and foreign minister, met in Rome with two top Soviet Middle East advisers — Karen Brutents and Alexander Zotov — and in July a Soviet consular mission arrived in Tel Aviv. In May 1988, Peres met with Yuri Dubinin, the Soviet ambassador to Washington, who presented a verbal proposal that went to great lengths to accommodate Israeli concerns, and in June at the UN, Prime Minister Shamir met with Shevardnadze and secured his approval of the posting of an Israeli consular mission to Moscow. That delegation arrived the following month, thereby reestablishing an official Israeli presence in the Soviet Union. In December, Shevardnadze received Aryeh Levin, the head of the Israeli mission, to thank him for Israel's cooperation in returning the hijackers of a Soviet aircraft, but he used the opportunity to discuss political relations, which were formally beyond the scope of the mission's responsibilities.

In 1989, Shevardnadze met three times with the new Israeli foreign minister, Moshe Arens, in January at the Paris conference on chemical weapons, in February during Shevardnadze's visit to Cairo, and in September at the UN. That year Shimon Peres (then vice prime minister and finance minister) also held several high-level meetings, including another one with Karen Brutents, the head of the International Department. All of these meetings were held on "neutral" ground, but in November the Israeli minister of agriculture made the first ministerial visit to Moscow, though officially as a guest of the Soviet Academy of Sciences rather than of the Soviet government. A high-level government visit did not take place until January 1990, when Science and Technology Minister Ezer Weizman met with Shevardnadze. During the course of the year, he was followed by the minister of religious affairs, the minister of housing and construction, and, in September, by the ministers of finance (Yitzhak Moda'i) and of science and technology (Yuval Ne'eman), who had the first official Israeli meeting with Gorbachev. At the end of September, Shevardnadze met with Israeli Foreign Minister David Levy at the UN, and the two agreed to establish full consular relations and open separate consulates-general. And in December, after a meeting with Prime Minister Yitzhak Shamir at the UN, Shevardnadze announced that the Soviet Union no longer placed any preconditions on the renewal of diplomatic relations at the ambassadorial level.

Thus, by the end of 1990 the only elements still missing were a formal decision and the appointment of ambassadors. When Shevardnadze's successor, Alexandr Bessmertnykh, made the first visit to Israel of a Soviet foreign minister in May 1991, there were expectations that these last elements would fall into place, but Bessmertnykh declared only that this would happen soon.

The same purposeful expansion of ties took place in other fields. The most important, from Israel's point of view, was increasing Jewish emigration. From a paltry 914 in 1986, the number grew to 7,776 in 1987 and 19,343 in 1988.[5] In 1989 it exceeded 40,000 and in 1990 it exploded to over 200,000. Due to aggravated economic hardship and political uncertainty, the monthly rate of emigration accelerated sharply toward the end of the year, when it was equivalent to an annual emigration of almost 500,000.

The revolution in emigration policy was accompanied by a change in attitudes to the development and expression of Jewish identity within the Soviet Union. The jamming of Israeli radio broadcasts ended in 1987 and, contrary to previous practices, the government permitted the opening of Jewish cultural centers, the public teaching of Hebrew, the import of Jewish religious and cultural materials (including an Israeli book fair in Moscow), and open activity of local and foreign Jewish teachers, religious leaders and community organizers.

In the commercial field, ties were also intensified. The growth in travel, for example, was not confined to Jewish emigrants; by 1988, over 25,000 people were already traveling between the two countries, and this prompted representatives of Aeroflot and El Al to begin discussions on a commercial agreement in early January 1989.[6] In the same month, a Soviet-Swiss investment company based in Zurich invited 15 Israeli entrepreneurs to examine possibilities of economic cooperation.[7] In his capacity as finance minister, Shimon Peres discussed trade matters in most of his meetings. Further probes included meetings between the Soviet Chamber of Trade and Commerce and the Israeli Federation of Chambers of Commerce, culminating in a trade agreement signed in Moscow in early 1990 which put a formal end to the 23-year break in economic relations. This facilitated such an acceleration of commercial and technological agreements that they soon ceased to be noteworthy.[8]

In early June, during a summit meeting in Washington, Gorbachev himself even floated the idea of US-Soviet-Israeli joint production of aircraft, and a top Soviet trade official arrived in Israel at the end of the month to discuss the project.[9] The same was true in the academic, athletic and cultural fields; reciprocal visits by tourists, journalists, artists, scientific and other scholarly delegations, sports teams, theater companies, even rock stars and circuses, became altogether routine. At the beginning of 1989, the deputy head of the KGB even announced that he was interested in cooperating with the Mossad against terrorism.[10] In short, within the space of a few years, Soviet-Israeli ties had become almost normalized; there was virtually a full range of relations apart from the posting of ambassadors, in contrast to the pre-1967 situation, when there were ambassadors but virtually no other relations of any kind.

The change in Soviet-Israeli and Soviet-Jewish relations was partly attributable to the general desire to improve the Soviet image in the West; a major theme in Soviet analyses was that the Soviet Union had become a normal state engaged in normal international relations. However, Soviet officials were also interested in exploring opportunities for commercial access to technology and credit in Israel itself or in the West through Israeli or Jewish intermediaries (who were assumed to have great influence in western financial and media circles). This is why Soviet diplomats cultivated Jewish businessmen-activists such as Edgar Bronfman, with whom Ambassador Dubinin and Foreign Minister Shevardnadze both met in 1988 to discuss political matters.[11] In early 1990, a visiting Soviet trade mission expressed a strong interest in hosting an economic delegation, specifically mentioning Robert Maxwell, Nissim Ga'on, Armand Hammer, Shaul Eisenberg, and Ya'acov Taman as those whom it would like included.[12]

Nevertheless, the Soviet-Israeli bilateral relationship could not be isolated from overall Soviet policy on the Arab-Israel conflict. Diplomatic contacts with Israel (or other Jewish dignitaries) invariably addressed the procedures and sometimes the substance of a peace settlement and there was a perceptible softening of the Soviet position, particularly with respect to the international conference (and, by extension, to Soviet terms for a full restoration of diplomatic relations). In 1986 and 1987 Peres' foreign policy adviser, Nimrod Novik, held several meetings with Soviet officials in the course of which the structure and functions of the proposed conference were watered down to the point where it would constitute little more than an umbrella for direct negotiations in bilateral working teams. In the May 1988 "verbal paper" given to Foreign Minister Peres, the Soviets emphasized the "non-coercive" nature of the conference, adding that any Israeli withdrawal should be from "territories" (rather than "the territories") and intimating that Palestinian self-determination might be achieved in some framework other than a fully independent state.[13]

At the end of May, the spokesman of the International Department explicitly told an Israeli newspaper that Israel did not have to accept the Soviet version of an international conference, and in the December 1988 meeting between Shevardnadze and Levin, the former solicited Israeli suggestions for alternatives to an international conference.[14]

Indeed, subsequent endorsement of such mechanisms as preparatory multilateral meetings or preliminary bilateral contacts between Israel and Palestinians (such as those promoted by Secretary of State Baker and Egyptian President Mubarak in an effort to operationalize the Israeli government proposal of May 1989), suggested that the Soviets, to the extent that they continued to insist on an international conference at all, would be satisfied with a ceremonial opening symbolizing their own ostensibly coequal status with the United States. By early 1990 the Soviets were reported in Arab media to have completely waived the idea of a conference in favor of direct negotiations.[15] These developments were accompanied by recurrent declarations by the most senior Soviet leaders, including Gorbachev himself, to the effect that the Soviet Union bore no inherent hostility toward Israel and was sensitive to its legitimate security concerns.[16]

Meanwhile the traditional picture of Israel projected by Soviet propaganda came in for growing criticism. In early 1989, for example, an article in *Izvestia*, though generally sympathetic to the Palestinians, accused the Soviet press of relying on biased and misleading stereotypes in its coverage of the Israeli-Palestinian conflict, and in November 1989 Radomir Bogdanov, deputy president of the Soviet Peace Committee, attacked the systematic distortion of Israel's image in the Soviet media.[17] Instead, Soviet media began to provide more balanced, even sympathetic coverage of Israel, so much so that Arab corespondents in Moscow, responding to a series of articles in *Ogonyok*, felt obliged to lodge a public protest, and a Cairo newspaper expressed open concern about the impact of Jewish-Zionist activity on the Soviet media.[18] Finally, Soviet diplomacy ended its knee-jerk support for every pro-Arab or anti-Israel proposal in international forums: in May 1989 the Soviet Union voted against the PLO's admission to the World Health Organization; in October it abstained (for the first time since 1982) on the annual Arab motion to reject Israel's credentials in the UN General Assembly; and in November it refused to support the upgrading of the PLO's status at the United Nations to that of observer-state.

Not surprisingly, these changes in Soviet posture led to friction with various Arab parties, especially the closest Soviet allies — Syria and the PLO — who were subjected to increasingly pointed exhortations to abandon any illusions about military options and to moderate their political stances. The tone of Asad's second visit to Gorbachev, in 1987, was quite different from the first. The formal joint statement, in keeping with tradition, denounced imperialism and Zionism and called for a "full-fledged and plenipotentiary international conference" to establish peace on the basis of complete Israeli withdrawal and the creation of an independent Palestinian state; the Soviets also forgave 25 percent of Syria's military debt and agreed, finally, to supply a squadron of MiG-29 fighter aircraft, already sold to Iraq and India and offered to Jordan and Zimbabwe(!). But Gorbachev (or, by some accounts, Shevardnadze) also declared at a state dinner that there was no military solution to the conflict and that the absence of ties between the Soviet Union and Israel was not normal.[19] Asad received the same political message in an oft-postponed return visit in April 1990.

Meanwhile, the military and financial dimensions of new political thinking were being conveyed to other Syrian officials in rather striking terms. When Defense Minister Mustafa Tlas visited Moscow in October 1988, he reportedly failed to get either new weapons or a waiver of the remaining debt.[20] Following reports of very serious tensions in Soviet-Syrian relations, Marshal Yazov went to Damascus in March 1989 (on the first visit of a Soviet defense minister in 19 years) and reportedly responded to some of Syria's longstanding requests for more advanced armaments, including a second squadron of MiG-29s and a limited number of Su-24 attack bombers, but he again refused to write off the remaining debt and made it clear that continuing defense ties did not imply Soviet support for the Syrian goal of strategic parity.[21] Finally, the Soviet refusal to supply particularly sensitive weapons systems which the Syrians had repeatedly requested, such as the SS-23 surface-to-surface missile, was constant and unyielding. Syrian concerns were further aroused in late 1989 and early 1990, when Soviet Ambassador Alexander Zotov stressed publicly that Soviet aid was limited to "reasonable defensive sufficiency" and emphasized that the Soviet-Syrian treaty of 1980 did not oblige the Soviet Union to take part in Syria's wars.[22] Incidentally, before his appointment to Damascus, Zotov, then a senior Middle East specialist attached to the International Department, had told a visiting British Foreign Office delegation that "Israel has been a natural partner of the USSR since 1947."[23]

From 1985 to 1989 Soviet arms deliveries, in constant 1987 dollars, averaged $1.3 billion per year, as opposed to $2.9 billion in 1980-84, and at the end of 1989, American intelligence agencies reportedly monitored a further, discernible reduction in the flow of weaponry to Syria.[24] To some extent, this trend may just have been fortuitous. Massive arms deliveries in 1982 and 1983 were dictated by the urgent need to replace and upgrade Syrian air force and air defense equipment destroyed during the Lebanon War, and it is unlikely that arms transfers could have continued at that pace under any circumstances. Nevertheless, the political context and the specific content of Soviet-Syrian discussions clearly reflect a conscious reassessment of Soviet attitudes toward Syrian force planning and policy.

The PLO also came in for its share of advice, particularly about the need to adopt a more realistic and flexible position. Despite consistent rhetorical support, Gorbachev had shown little enthusiasm for or interest in the PLO; when Yasir Arafat came to attend the 70th anniversary celebrations of the Bolshevik Revolution in 1987, he was met at the airport by a cosmonaut, and during his stay in Moscow, Gorbachev could spare only 10 minutes to talk to him.[25] When Arafat finally did pay an official visit in April 1988, he was told by Gorbachev that any settlement of the conflict required recognition of Israel and consideration of its security needs.[26] And in the fall of that year, in anticipation of the upcoming session of the Palestine National Council in Algiers, PLO leaders were urged by senior Foreign Ministry and International Department officials not to alienate Israeli or American opinion by taking ill-considered actions, such as unilaterally declaring a state or forming a government-in-exile.[27] Soviet spokesmen claimed some credit for the actual resolutions of the PNC and for the subsequent clarifications by Yasir Arafat in Geneva and Stockholm that made possible the beginning of a US-PLO dialogue, which the Soviets actually encouraged; through the zero-sum prism of old thinking, this development would have been seen as a setback to Soviet interests.

The Soviets also became increasingly vocal in their criticism of Palestinian terrorism. Though they consistently declared their opposition to terrorism in general, the Soviets until early 1989 remained reluctant to categorize anything done by Palestinians (or other Arabs) to Israelis as terrorism (for which the Soviets were themselves often criticized by American officials).[28] But after a Palestinian from Gaza deliberately crashed a Jerusalem-bound bus in July that year and killed 16 people, Soviet media denounced the "despicable terrorist act" and attacked Palestinians and Syrians who took a more understanding or approving position. A year later Radio Moscow commentators, on two separate occasions, responded to the killing of three Israelis in a Jerusalem residential area by condemning the "vicious and despicable" terrorist attacks on Jews by Palestinians.[29]

Despite the frictions engendered by these political changes, the most neuralgic issue in Soviet-Arab relations by 1990 had become the question of Jewish immigration. In the first half of the year Soviet officials, journalists and ordinary citizens were bombarded by strident condemnations from almost every Arab quarter. The criticism itself was ground in a variety of concerns: the expectation that Jewish immigrants would be settled in the occupied territories, the fear that the demographic impact in Israel would profoundly change the overall Israeli-Arab balance of power, and the belief that it betrayed an irreversible Soviet tilt toward Israel, perhaps as part of an American-Soviet conspiracy to take control of the Middle East at the expense of the Arabs. But whatever the reason, the Soviets found themselves on the defensive and tried to respond by a combination of explanation (that the free emigration of Soviet citizens was part of democratization and had nothing to do with Jews or Arabs per se), reassurance (that the numbers leaving were vastly exaggerated), and warnings (to Israel, not to direct Soviet Jews to the occupied territories). What is significant, however, is that beyond these themes, there was also an element of counterattack in the way that various Soviet figures dealt with the issue; while denying that Soviet Jews in any significant numbers were settling in the Territories, some officials accused the Arabs of artificially stirring up a tempest, and others made the even more telling point that Arab states themselves had sent far more Jews to Israel than the Soviet Union ever would.[30] It was even suggested on at least one occasion that since the main reason so many Jews were leaving the Soviet Union was the deteriorating economic situation there, the rich Arab states could alleviate the problem by investing in Soviet economic reconstruction.[31]

The immigration issue continued to dominate Soviet-Arab relations until it was eclipsed by the Iraqi invasion of Kuwait. But by that time, it had, together with the other difficulties and frictions discussed, produced an attitude of widespread disillusionment, despair and anger among the Soviet Union's allies and friends in the Arab world. This sentiment was undoubtedly felt throughout the Arab world, particularly on the issue of Jewish immigration, but the greatest resentment was expressed by traditional Soviet friends and allies in the radical camp, the Palestinians first of all. In March 1990, for example, Palestinians staged a sit-in demonstration in front of the Soviet Embassy in Algiers.[32] And it was a member of the PLO Executive Committee, Abdallah Hourani, who gave most poignant expression to the general mood when he told the Tunis daily *As-Sabah*, "It is no longer possible to regard Moscow as a friend and ally of world forces of liberation, including the Arab world and the Palestinian people and cause."[33]

Elsewhere in the Arab world, the developing Soviet rapprochement with Israel did not preclude implementation of another principle of new political thinking: the diversification of relations with states regardless of their ideological orientation. In political terms, the most significant development was the progressive rehabilitation of relations with Egypt as that country reemerged as a major center of power in the Arab world after several years of relative isolation following the peace treaty with Israel. Soviet-Egyptian ties had been formally renewed in 1984, before Gorbachev assumed office. But in April 1987 the Soviet Union agreed to waive the interest due on Egypt's military debt and to stretch out the principal repayments over 25 years. By early 1988 there were reports that the Soviets had agreed to renew the military supply relationship, mostly in the form of sales of spare parts, and during the course of the year, Soviet cultural centers and consulates were reopened in Egypt and new agreements on trade, technical and scientific cooperation were signed. During the visit by Shevardnadze to Cairo in February 1989, a joint economic commission was established to promote trade, but in April 1990 Egypt suspended exports because the Soviets had already built up a large deficit (180 million pounds sterling) and could offer nothing in return.[34] However, during President Mubarak's visit to Moscow in May, a new 10-year trade agreement was signed and Mubarak became the first foreign leader to address the Supreme Soviet, signaling the full rehabilitation of relations.

In addition to offers of advanced weaponry, the device which facilitated Egyptian-Soviet rapprochement — rescheduling of a military debt — was also utilized to enhance relations with Jordan, though in this case the amount was relatively small; in February 1990, the Soviet side agreed to stretch out repayment on $168 million and accept most of the balance in goods.[35] Even in Lebanon, the Soviets diversified their ties by pursuing visible contacts with previously-shunned elements, such as General Michel Aoun, the "prime minister" of the Christian enclave and the most outspoken anti-Syrian leader in the country.[36] In the Gulf, the quest for universal ties was facilitated by the declining threat from local communist parties, and persistent Soviet efforts to ingratiate themselves with Gulf regimes were rewarded in 1985 when Oman and the United Arab Emirates agreed to establish diplomatic relations in September and November, respectively.[37] Relations with Kuwait had long been on a sound basis, and developments appeared to vindicate the policy of cultivating capitalist, western-oriented states: in July 1988 Kuwait made a large purchase ($300 million) of Soviet military equipment; in February 1989 an agreement was signed on joint enterprises to develop oil facilities in the Soviet Union; and in May 1990 the Kuwait Foreign Investments and Contracting Company agreed to lend $300 million to the Soviet Bank for Foreign Trade.[38]

However, the biggest prize — Saudi Arabia — was more elusive.

Saudi Arabia and the Soviet Union began a cautious diplomatic minuet in the summer of 1985, when the head of the Saudi Higher Council for Youth and Sports made the first visit of a Saudi official (except for members of multinational delegations). The first ministerial visit took place in January 1987, when the Saudi oil minister met with Shevardnadze in Moscow. A year later Saud al-Faisal made the first separate visit of a Saudi foreign minister, and the pace of contacts then intensified. In February 1988 Vladimir Poliakov, the head of the Middle East Department in the Foreign Ministry, made the first high-level Soviet visit to Saudi Arabia. These contacts focused on two issues, the Soviet reluctance to approve an arms embargo against Iran and the Soviet presence in Afghanistan. The clear implication — signaled by Qatar's agreement in August 1988 to establish formal ties — was that when those problems were overcome, there would be no further obstacles to a renewal of diplomatic relations. The end of the Iran-Iraq War rendered the first problem moot; Soviet withdrawal from Afghanistan eliminated the second. As a result, there was little excitement or surprise when the Saudi foreign minister traveled to Moscow in September 1990 and agreed to the formal restoration of diplomatic ties. Two months later, the de-ideologization of Soviet policy paid off, in the form of a Saudi loan of almost $4 billion.

The two major elements in new political thinking on the Middle East — withdrawal of support for radical, militant approaches to regional conflicts and the cultivation of capitalist, economically-useful partners — appeared to come together in the Soviet response to the first major Middle East crisis of the post-Cold War era, the Iraqi invasion of Kuwait in August 1990. If the rules of old political thinking had still been in effect, the Soviet role would probably have evolved, with almost mechanical predictability, according to the following script: the Soviets would have maintained close military and political ties with the Iraqi regime right up until the invasion, would have strenuously tried to dissuade Saddam Hussein from actually crossing the border in force (if they had known about his plans), would have failed in their endeavors but would in any event have continued to support him afterward, working to orchestrate a "progressive" coalition in the region, justifying his claims against Kuwait, seconding his efforts to link imperialism and Zionism, condemning the United States and its reactionary allies for exploiting the crisis in order to introduce their armed forces into a region close to the southern borders of the Soviet Union, and blocking any action on sanctions in the UN Security Council. There would have been naval and military maneuvers, a rise in tensions, perhaps even some isolated incidents, a crisis in Soviet-American relations, fears of escalation, and then, perhaps, a political arrangement leaving Iraq with some profit, the region itself more polarized and unstable, and the Soviet Union with a formal gain and a much worse relationship with the United States.

In fact, Soviet-Iraqi cooperation did continue right up to the eve of the invasion; on July 29, Soviet Minister of Defense Industry Boris Belousov left Baghdad after signing minutes of an agreement on joint industrial and technical cooperation.[39] But in almost every other respect, the subsequent course of events was altogether different.

The Soviet Union immediately denounced the Iraqi action, cut off further arms shipments, and supported UN resolutions to condemn Iraq and impose economic sanctions, despite the fact that these measures entailed costs of several billion dollars in lost trade and debt recovery.[40] Moreover, the Soviets did nothing to obstruct American-led efforts to prepare the political and operational groundwork for military action against Iraq. On the morrow of the invasion, Shevardnadze and Secretary of State Baker issued a joint statement in Moscow condemning "this blatant transgression of the basic norms of civilized conduct" and calling for unconditional Iraqi withdrawal and the restoration of the sovereignty, independence, legitimate authorities, and territorial integrity of Kuwait.[41] In mid-August, Gorbachev told officers of the Black Sea Fleet that the Iraqi invasion was "an act of treachery and a blatant violation of international law and the UN Charter," and in the joint communique following the Helsinki Summit with President Bush, he agreed that nothing short of the restoration of the pre-August 2 status quo was acceptable, and that if all peaceful efforts failed to achieve this, he was prepared "to consider additional ones consistent with the UN Charter."[42] And in late

November, the Soviet Union voted in favor of Security Council Resolution 678, which authorized the use of "all necessary means" if Iraq had not withdrawn by January 15, 1991. By some accounts, the Soviet Union even offered logistical and intelligence support for the western military deployment in Saudi Arabia.[43] With these actions, the Soviet Union found itself aligned with the United States, the major NATO powers, and their most important Arab allies (Saudi Arabia and Egypt), and against traditional Soviet partners such as the PLO, South Yemen (now united with Yemen), Libya, and Cuba.

It is difficult to imagine a more convincing affirmation of the revolutionary transformation in Soviet Third World policy. Rather than viewing the Third World as an arena for zero-sum competition with the United States (and, hence, having its posture virtually dictated by the established global orientation of local belligerents), the Soviet Union now appeared determined to promote a cooperative relationship with the United States (and with conservative or status quo regional powers such as Saudi Arabia) and to fashion its policies on regional conflicts primarily with this aim in mind.

The magnitude of this transformation was so great that one factor in Saddam Hussein's calculus may well have been an inability to believe that it had actually taken place. While active Soviet neutralization of the United States could no longer be automatically assumed, Saddam probably did not act with this assumption in mind, since he had little reason to believe that it would be necessary; given American behavior before the invasion, the vigor of the American reaction was itself almost certainly unexpected. However, Saddam could have anticipated some continuing Soviet support, or at worst Soviet passivity; that the Soviet Union would become an active partner in a US-led effort to impose an arms embargo and diplomatic and economic sanctions, and even to provide some military assistance to the US (in the form of intelligence) probably seemed too swift, radical and improbable a departure from the historical thrust of Soviet policy in the region. If so, then Saddam's incredulity was not entirely without foundation. For the transformation of Soviet behavior in the Middle East was neither as steady nor as unambiguous as a static and superficial comparison of 1984 and 1990/91 might suggest.

Even after the basic contours of policy on the Gulf crisis had been established, important differences of approach with the United States remained. The Soviets were among the first to close their embassy in Kuwait. Soviet official military advisers and technicians were not immediately withdrawn from Iraq, though this was quite probably a result of Iraq's refusal to let them (along with most other foreigners) leave at the outset of the crisis. Still, Soviet spokesmen did not focus on the "hostage" dimension of this issue, instead issuing confusing or misleading statements about the advisers' numbers and functions. Soviet spokesmen also exhorted the United States not to act unilaterally, were much more categorical in opposing the use of force against Iraq (and later urged that the beginning of the ground war be delayed), maintained continuous diplomatic contacts with Iraq in an active pursuit of a political settlement (unlike the western or Arab members of the coalition, who agreed to meet directly with Iraq only after the Security Council resolution authorizing the use of force had been passed), tended to depict extra-regional intervention as a regrettable and temporary expedient until such time as an "Arab solution" (which they favored) could be found, were less unequivocal in rejecting the Iraqi idea of establishing procedural and substantive links between the Gulf crisis and the Israeli-Palestinian conflict, and stressed their concern that the US-led coalition not exceed the UN mandate and inflict excessive damage on Iraq.

This track of Soviet diplomacy was pursued by veteran orientalist and presidential foreign policy adviser Yevgeny Primakov, who undertook three separate mediation efforts. Primakov frequently urged that Saddam be allowed to save face and it was suggested that he attempted to forestall a war by offering Saddam Hussein some kind of reward in exchange for withdrawal from Kuwait — either the islands of Warbah and Bubayan and part of a Kuwaiti oilfield, or more explicit linkage to the Arab-Israel conflict. The first charge, made by Novosti after his trip to Baghdad in October 1990, was vociferously denied by Primakov;[44] the second could not be, because the idea of linkage was explicitly or implicitly endorsed on several occasions by others in the Soviet hierarchy, including the foreign minister and the president himself.[45] American officials did, however, remark that Primakov consistently accentuated anything positive that the Iraqis might say while playing down their inflexibility.[46] Of course, Primakov did not act on his own authority. The most dramatic manifestation of the Soviet proclivity to pursue a distinct (though not contradictory) policy was Gorbachev's own direct intervention in late February, in a futile attempt to avert a ground war.

These nuances in Soviet behavior led some observers to suspect that the Soviet Union, for all its cooperation, was hoping to leave itself better positioned than the United States to cultivate preferred relations with the Arab world (including Iraq) after the Gulf crisis ended.[47] Furthermore, occasional nonauthoritative statements reflected the persistence of other elements of old political thinking. At the end of August 1990, for example, Deputy Foreign Minister Alexander Belonogov declared his concern that US forces might not leave Saudi Arabia after the crisis, and Warsaw Pact Chief-of-Staff General Vladimir Lobov worried that those forces might actually be extended along the Soviet southern flank in order to put pressure on Moscow.[48] Although these statements were later rebuked by the Foreign Ministry spokesman, Soviet conservatives, especially among the Soyuz bloc of parliamentary deputies, attacked the government for planning to participate in a military campaign against Iraq (which government spokesmen repeatedly and vehemently denied) and criticized the leadership in general, and the Foreign Ministry in particular, for being too subservient to American wishes.[49]

Such expressions of discomfort with the implications of new political thinking were not isolated occurrences. Instead, they were simply the latest and perhaps least significant vestiges of ambivalence about, and even resistance to the adoption and implementation of its logic. Earlier and far more compelling evidence that the competitive, zero-sum paradigm of Soviet-American relations could not easily be discarded came from the Iran-Iraq War, especially during 1987-88, just when new thinking in other areas was gaining real momentum. Unlike the Israel-Arab conflict, the Soviets in this case did not bear the burden of an established, exclusive commitment to one side in the conflict. Nor did their definition of the conflict's utility in global terms dictate a preference for one side or the other; their longstanding objective was to cultivate both while avoiding the defeat of either. This objective coincided with the American aim, and both superpowers did pursue essentially parallel balance-preservation policies for most of the war, meaning a slight tilt toward the seemingly more vulnerable side: Iran until 1982, Iraq thereafter. By the mid-1980s, Soviet collaboration with the United States to pressure the more intransigent of the belligerents — at that point, Iran — to accept a political compromise and end the fighting would not have damaged their regional standing or any intrinsic interests, and might well have facilitated superpower conciliation in other areas. Nevertheless, the Soviets succumbed to a seemingly-irresistible opportunity to make gains at American expense, especially in Iran, while offering themselves as mediators in any negotiations to end the war.[50]

To a large extent, of course, this objective had guided Soviet policy on Iran since the overthrow of the Shah. It is also true that the American "arms-for-hostages" deal with Iran was rationalized, if not explained, by the hope of finding Iranian "moderates" with whom the United States could cooperate to resist the dangers of Soviet penetration, and that exposure of these dealings in late 1986 could only be interpreted by the Soviets as a new American determination to compete for influence in Iran. However, the Soviets actively promoted industrial, commercial and military ties with Iran even in 1985-86 — after the initial threat of Iraqi victory had passed, after the Soviets had resumed armed sales to Iraq, after Iran had rejected any settlement apart from Iraqi surrender and the most widely-anticipated outcome of the war had become an Iranian victory, but before American-Iranian contacts had been revealed. Soviet actions therefore helped postpone the day when Iran would be forced to concede that it could not win a war of attrition.

In April 1985 for example, Iranian Deputy Foreign Minister Kazembur Ardabili traveled to Moscow and came back with overflight rights for Iran Air and promises of more technical assistance; a year before, the Soviets had agreed to construct power plants in Iran.[51] There were reports that during his visit,

Ardabili also met a Col.-Gen. Sergeichik, with whom he discussed long-term plans for building a defense infrastructure in Iran.[52] At this time Gorbachev, barely a month in office, was probably unaware of and almost certainly uninterested in such meetings, and Gromyko was still foreign minister. In February 1986, however, Gorbachev had been in office for almost a year and Shevardnadze had taken over the Foreign Ministry when his first deputy, Georgi Kornienko, traveled to Tehran to discuss oil and bilateral economic relations and to resume Aeroflot service to Iran. In August both the deputy foreign minister and the oil minister of Iran were in Moscow to discuss, among other things, the resumption of Iranian natural gas exports to the Soviet Union.[53] Thus the October 1986 revelation about American-Iranian contacts only accelerated a process that had already been going on. In December the first meeting of the Joint Soviet-Iranian Economic Commission since 1979 took place in Iran, and a protocol was signed covering several economic issues, including natural gas deliveries.[54] And in February 1987, Iranian Foreign Minister Ali Akhbar Velayati made the highest-ranking visit to the Soviet Union since the Islamic Revolution.

This process of Soviet-Iranian reconciliation provides the background for Soviet policy during the "end game" of the war, from the American decision to "reflag" Kuwaiti tankers in March 1987 until the ceasefire in August 1988.[55] Given the primary reason for the American reflagging decision — to preempt a similar Soviet move — it is hardly surprising that the Soviets were not overly supportive of American efforts to end the war. Instead, they tried to preempt an American-sponsored Security Council resolution by proposing a ceasefire in the tanker war (which would objectively favor Iran).[56] Only when that failed, in July 1987, did they reluctantly support Resolution 598, which called for a general ceasefire and a withdrawal to international borders. However, they continued to resist American efforts for a "follow-on" resolution authorizing mandatory sanctions against any side which failed to comply. Throughout 1987 and 1988 they protected Iran from such a resolution, instead supporting Iranian proposals like the demand for an inquiry into the responsibility for the war and bringing about a "mini-crisis" in relations with Iraq, now quite openly identified with the United States.[57] During this period, the major theme in Soviet declarations on the war was the condemnation of the American naval presence in the Gulf. And when Iraq resumed the "war of the cities" in February 1988, the Soviets introduced an emergency UN resolution calling for an end to attacks on civilian targets; this was supported by Iran, but opposed by Iraq and the United States.[58] The last attempt to gain an advantage at American expense was a reported offer by First Deputy Foreign Minister Yuli Vorontsov, two days after the ceasefire had been accepted but before it had gone into effect, to hold peace talks in "a Soviet Muslim city."[59]

After the war, Soviet-Iranian rapprochement intensified, though more in the context of the general Soviet diplomatic posture focused on mutually beneficial economic relations than as part of the superpower competition. In November, political and economic relations were again discussed in Tehran, this time between First Deputy Foreign Minister Bessmertnykh and Parliament Speaker Hashemi Rafsanjani, and by January 1989 relations had reached the point where Gorbachev received an emissary from Ayatollah Khomeini, with a letter urging Gorbachev to acknowledge the failure of communism and undertake a serious study of Islam. Whatever its spiritual impact, the letter paved the way for a series of high-level contacts, including Shevardnadze's audience with Khomeini in February (the first ever granted to a visiting foreign minister). The steady expansion of commercial and technological ties culminated in Rafsanjani's June visit to Moscow, where he negotiated a package of economic agreements reportedly valued at $15 billion and secured a Soviet commitment to supply weapons and assistance for Iranian military industries. And in early 1990, natural gas shipments — the subject of so many consultations since 1986 — were finally renewed after a 10-year hiatus.[60] But even the apparent regulation of ties with Iran on a commercial, non-ideological basis did not rule out an occasional attempt to highlight the difference between the Soviet Union and the United States; on a visit to Iran in September 1990, Deputy Foreign Minister Belonogov made a point of reminding his hosts that the Soviet Union, too, was unhappy about the buildup of foreign forces in the Gulf.[61]

Inconsistency in the application of new political thinking in the Middle East was not confined to the Iran-Iraq War or (albeit in a far less cogent manner) to Soviet responses to the Iraqi invasion of Kuwait. Despite Soviet interest in regional arms control, the demilitarization of foreign policy did not preclude the sale of destabilizing weapons systems to destabilizing regimes. In April 1989, for example, US intelligence sources reported the delivery of six Su-24 bombers to Libya. Soviet spokesmen initially denied the report, then confirmed that the aircraft had indeed been sold, but that they were not equipped with mid-air refuelling capability and that the delivery represented overdue fulfillment of a contract signed in 1986 (or 1982).[62] More generally, there was no palpable reduction in military assistance to traditional clients such as Syria and Iraq (apart from declining weapons sales, which were in most cases due to declining effective demand). From 1985 to 1990, for example, the number of Soviet military advisers and technicians in Iraq, Libya, Syria and Yemen dropped only slightly, from 6,000 to 4,700, and even that decline was partly counterbalanced by the large number of nonuniformed experts — almost 800, according to Congressman Les Aspin — working in Iraqi military industries on the eve of the invasion of Kuwait.[63] Nor did the Soviet government always refrain from trying to derail developments that held out some promise of progress toward a political settlement of the Arab-Israel conflict but might work to the benefit of the United States or western-aligned forces in the region. Like the 1978 Camp David Agreements, the Hussein-Arafat Agreement of 1985 was vigorously criticized as a vehicle for a "separate accord," which the Soviets made every effort to undermine.[64]

Even with respect to bilateral Soviet-Israel relations, where perhaps the most dramatic transformation took place, there were nevertheless recurrent indications of resistance to change and persistence of old attitudes. The fact that in 1989 the Soviets stopped voting to reject Israel's credentials in the UN General Assembly only highlights the fact that during the first three years of new political thinking they did vote to reject, a practice which the Foreign Ministry spokesman tried to dismiss as "just a voting tradition."[65] Moreover, the normally more balanced discussion of Israel and the Arab-Israel conflict was occasionally still marred by the tone and terminology of the pre-Gorbachev era. In 1987, for example, *World Economy and International Relations*, the journal of the similarly-named institute (IMEMO) which was generally a stalwart of new political thinking, published an article on the Palestinian movement replete with archaic-sounding praise of progressive forces and attacks on imperialism and Zionism "endeavoring to weaken and emasculate the anti-imperialist content of this [Palestinian] struggle as much as possible."[66] In the age of glasnost, the use of these categories of analysis did not necessarily reflect government or Party policy anymore, but official statements also continued to make use of them. As late as 1990, the Soviet ambassador to South Yemen, Veniamin Popov, wrote an article in a San'a newspaper in which he explained that "part of the problem [of Jewish emigration] has to do with Tel Aviv's illegitimate acts and its persisting expansionism, which has US backing."[67] Despite growing traffic and lost revenues, high-level Soviet leaders prevented implementation of the El Al-Aeroflot agreement of October 1989 to institute regular direct flights between the two countries. The most blatant case of old thinking, of course, was the Soviet refusal to reestablish full diplomatic relations.

If the persistence of some old patterns raised questions about the comprehensiveness of new political thinking in the Middle East, the newness of some its elements was not always obvious, either. In fact, there were significant continuities with pre-1985 behavior, even if Soviet policy was carried out with greater flexibility and sophistication. For example, the diversification of relations with conservative, capitalist forces in the region, so prominent a feature of Soviet diplomacy after 1985, was hardly a doctrinal innovation. Its roots went back through Khrushchev's pursuit of anti-imperialist nationalists and Stalin's popular fronts to Lenin's endorsement of cooperation with the national bourgeoisie. Even in Brezhnev's time, the Soviet Union tried to expand ties with many of the same targets later reached by Gorbachev's envoys. In April 1981, for example, the indirect, commercial approach to the UAE was tried by means of a request by the Moscow Chamber of Commerce for floor space at a trade exhibition in Abu Dhabi.[68] In most cases, the successes achieved in this respect under Gorbachev were due more to greater receptiveness on the part of the wooed than to greater ardor on the part of the wooer.

The major exception in this respect was Israel, but even here the change, however far-reaching, was not totally without precedent. The same oft-cited desire for better relations with Israel that Gorbachev expressed at a dinner for Asad in 1987 was reportedly uttered by Brezhnev at a dinner for King Hussein in 1981.[69] For a while, even Jewish emigration was permitted by Brezhnev, on a rather large scale; beginning with a few in 1969, the total number of emigres had reached a quarter-million when a clampdown was imposed a decade later.[70] Not surprisingly, this first wave of emigration also led to strains with Arab allies; in April 1972, on the eve of a critical trip to Moscow, Egyptian President Sadat wrote to Brezhnev and lodged a strong complaint about the flow of Soviet immigrants to Israel.[71]

Finally, the purported centerpiece of new thinking on Third World conflicts — the desire to collaborate with the United States on their peaceful resolution — was a constant feature of Soviet policy long before Gorbachev. Indeed, it was central to Brezhnev's Middle East policy even before the inauguration of detente.[72] Soviet spokesmen cited approvingly the precedents of the 1973 Geneva Conference and the October 1977 Joint Communique, blaming the United States for the eventual barrenness of both these mechanisms, and even a highly-orthodox analysis of the Third World in the early 1980s concluded with a call for US-Soviet cooperation and joint efforts "to defuse explosive conflicts before they break out."[73] Thus, when President Reagan endorsed the idea of "periodic consultations at the policy level about regional problems" in his September 1984 address to the United Nations, he was in effect responding to a long-standing Soviet proposal, and the first of these consultations, devoted to the Middle East, took place in February 1985, a month before Gorbachev took office. The major difference since then, of course, has been the willingness of the Soviet Union to distance itself from its own allies in order to facilitate cooperative relations with the United States.

Indeed, Soviet policy under Gorbachev might even be described as incremental implementation of the conditions posed by the

American government in 1985 for Soviet involvement in the Arab-Israeli peace process: renewal of diplomatic relations with Israel, an end to anti-Semitic propaganda within the Soviet Union, an end to persecution of Soviet Jews (including those wishing to emigrate), a halt in arms shipments to various militias in Lebanon, an effort to influence Soviet allies to halt arms shipments to Iran, and an end to Soviet attempts to torpedo the Arab-Israeli peace process.[74] But while the substance of policy since 1985 may have been inspired by explicit American requirements, it was the willingness to comply with, or at least be guided by those requirements, i.e., the general determination to remove the Middle East (and the rest of the Third World) as a source of superpower friction, that explains the overall thrust of Soviet behavior. And the importance of that one difference is almost impossible to exaggerate.

The vague and even banal character of the principles of new political thinking, their incomplete and inconsistent application, the persistence of elements of traditional behavior in the Middle East, and the fact that ostensibly new approaches have their roots in previous periods have all given rise to some confusion and led to various explanations for these apparent contradictions. The following discussion will attempt to assess the most common of these.

1. *New Thinking is a Fraud*

A widespread feeling among western analysts, especially in the early years of the Gorbachev era, was that new political thinking really meant nothing other than more sophisticated rhetoric, more flexible tactics, and more skillful diplomacy. The historical record certainly justified skepticism, and for some time ambiguous evidence made it possible to construct a persuasive argument for this case. One of the most articulate expositions of continuity in Soviet "new imperial policy" concluded that "it takes a giant leap of faith to contemplate a major change in Soviet policy or outlook."[75] Others put forward the (nonfalsifiable) proposition that recent Soviet restraint was explained by the absence of sufficiently promising opportunities for active intervention.[76] However plausible such arguments may have been during Gorbachev's first year or two in office, when the Soviet leadership was itself perhaps uncertain about the course it intended to follow, they were no longer tenable at the end of the decade. By then, it was simply inconceivable that a leadership willing to democratize and pluralize domestic society, to withdraw from Afghanistan with only fig-leaf guarantees, to endorse arms control agreements with the most intrusive verification provisions, to accept large, asymmetrical cuts in conventional arms, and, most importantly, to acquiesce in and even help stimulate the downfall of communist regimes in Eastern Europe, the destruction of the Berlin Wall, the inclusion of a united Germany in NATO, and the dissolution of the Warsaw Pact, was nevertheless still intent on perpetrating a fraud in the Third World, even in the Middle East.

2. *Inattention/Inertia*

A somewhat more persuasive argument is that the top leadership did not take an intense, ongoing interest in Soviet Middle Eastern policy. Although it defined the main guidelines and would certainly monopolize decisionmaking on critical issues such as military intervention, it was far too preoccupied with other, more important issues to follow closely the interpretation of those guidelines and their translation into day-to-day behavior. It is therefore likely that these dimensions of policy were simply left to lower levels less enthusiastic about a radical break with the past. The Middle East, in particular, did not demand urgent attention because, whatever its prominence in global (i.e., Soviet-American) political terms, it had ceased to be a real drain on the Soviet treasury once arms sales had shifted to a largely cash basis. Moreover, there were still large outstanding debts, the recovery of which might be jeopardized if Soviet insensitivity to established Arab clients went beyond certain bounds.[77] In these circumstances, it was natural that countervailing considerations, especially moral appeals, could not resonate as strongly. But while inertia and inattention might explain continuity in the formulation and especially the implementation of certain less-critical dimensions of Middle East policy, they could hardly account for Soviet behavior on matters of critical global importance, such as the Gulf crisis of 1990/91.

3. *Domestic Factors*

Inattention by the top leadership is related to a third explanation, namely that domestic political factors made it difficult to push new thinking to its logical conclusion. Certain domestic forces, it is argued, resist innovation, distort the interpretation of Soviet interests and the implementation of reformist thinking, and provide new rationales for old policies.

Domestic sources of foreign policy include bureaucratic or institutional interests and the force of public opinion. The first is a familiar theme in analyses of Soviet policy, and there has been much speculation about the possible role of various bureaucratic factors in the evolution of Soviet policies in general, and in the Middle East in particular. The conventional wisdom, often applied to other great powers in addition to the Soviet Union, is that the mission of the security branch of the foreign policy establishment — the military — encourages a more activist, confrontational posture, whereas the mission of the diplomatic branch — the foreign ministry — evokes more conciliatory, universalist tendencies. In the Soviet case, the first tendency is presumably strengthened by the institutional and ideological biases of other organs such as the Party (especially the International Department) and the KGB.

Some evidence, of course, can be adduced to support this thesis, especially during the Gulf crisis of 1990-91. For example, Soviet military advisers in Iraq reportedly came "close to mutiny" when recalled home and were angry at being forced to abandon one of their most loyal allies "in its time of need."[78] And much of the subsequent criticism of Soviet cooperation with the United States came from military quarters or was published in the army newspaper, *Red Star*. The military was particularly anxious to dissociate itself institutionally from the actual campaign against Iraq, and the Chief-of-Staff, General Moiseyev, went to great lengths to deny all the reports concerning the provision of intelligence data about Iraq to the United States.[79] Furthermore, the mediation efforts of Primakov, according to some reports, were undertaken in response to pressure from the conservatives — among whom senior military officers were prominent — despite the opposition of Shevardnadze himself.[80] It is quite clear that differences of opinion about Soviet policy on the Gulf crisis emanated from competing world views, i.e., they were not just arguments about tactics, and that the traditional institutional values and/or interests of the military were echoed in the arguments of those who opposed the "betrayal" of Iraq and, in general, collaboration with the United States. Even at the outset of the crisis, suspicion that the armed forces might subvert declared policy was so strong that a Defense Ministry spokesmen had to deny a widely-circulated rumor that the commander of the mission in Iraq was one of the most prominent and outspoken of army hard-liners, General Albert Makashov.[81]

Nevertheless, it would be an oversimplification to attribute all vestiges of old thinking in Soviet policy to the army, as embodied in the senior command. At best, the army is but one element in a broader, often bizarre coalition including old-line party functionaries and Russian nationalists. Furthermore, at least insofar as the Arab-Israeli complex is concerned, the conventional wisdom on bureaucratic politics has been challenged by a contrary analysis, namely, that it is the growing influence of the Foreign Ministry in recent years and the proclivities of its leadership and professional staff (except, perhaps, for the minister himself) that have actually hampered and retarded the implementation of new political thinking.

Those Bolsheviks who expected the imminent triumph of the communist revolution in Europe were not overly concerned with the practices or niceties of professional diplomacy. The importance they attached to traditional institutions such as foreign ministries was reflected in Trotsky's explanation of why he agreed to become Commissar of Foreign Relations. "I myself took this," he said, "so I would have more time for Party work. All there is to do is to publish the secret treaties. Then I will close the shop."[82] However, the need to deal with foreign states in more conventional ways as well guaranteed the Foreign Ministry a role in the implementation, if not the formulation of Soviet foreign policy. This role was inevitably strengthened after 1985 when political alliances made the foreign minister a key political supporter and confidante of the Party leader (as was the case with Shevardnadze), and particularly when the emphasis on de-ideologization led to the downgrading of competing institutions, such as the International Department, and a greater demand for professionalism in the analysis of international affairs.

In the Middle East, however, greater Foreign Ministry influence was not necessarily conducive to the kind of innovation intrinsic to new political thinking, especially with respect to Israel. Like that of foreign ministries in other countries, the mission of Soviet foreign policy bureaucrats is to ensure good relations with those with whom they do business, and this often creates a propensity to empathize with, pander to, and advocate the views of governments or populations to whom they are accredited or with whom they deal, a phenomenon known as "clientilism." Because of the dense, highly-populated and longstanding network of Soviet channels to the Arab world, Israeli observers sometimes charge the Middle East Department of the Soviet Foreign Ministry with an "Arabist" world-view, inclined to delay or subvert improved ties with Israel in order to conciliate their own "clients."[83] It is not clear why the defense establishment, for example, should not be just as concerned about the possible loss of missions or postings in Arab states that might result from retrenchment in general, or better ties with Israel in particular. Nevertheless, the Foreign Ministry appears to be the strongest institutional retardant of full-fledged Soviet-Israeli rapprochement. For example, it was visibly involved on several occasions in delaying implementation of agreements on direct flights between Moscow and Tel Aviv.

This assessment of the ministry's role is not confined to Israelis alone. Soviet analysts have also commented on the tendency of "moribund officialdom" in the Foreign Ministry to base Middle East policy on "outworn stereotypes."[84] In apparent reference to senior Middle East officials in the ministry, a newspaper closely identified with the push for more radical implementation of new thinking worried about the fact that "the same incompetent people who were for decades involved in developing our foreign policy in this part of the world and made so many mistakes continue to have influence on the political decisionmaking apparatus."[85]

The response of Foreign Ministry spokesman Gennadi Gerasimov to a question about the Gorbachev-Moda'i/Ne'eman meeting a day before it took place — that he didn't know about it but thought that such a meeting was highly unlikely — suggests that the ministry may be, if not hostile to, at least out of touch with the inclinations of the top political leadership. Conversely, there is evidence of promptings from outside the ministry for it to move faster than it was inclined to do; Shevardnadze himself criticized (unnamed) "voices" calling for old friends to be spurned or exchanged for new ones.[86]

Whatever the case, there is clearly a pluralism of views about the Arab-Israeli issue vying for preeminence. Furthermore, statements by ministry officials or diplomats and by others in the foreign policy establishment or on its periphery — such as media commentators and analysts in the research institutes of the Academy of Sciences (especially among "globalists" rather than those dealing with "oriental studies") — strongly suggest systematic differences in outlook that are most logically explained by professional socialization or institutional interests. On the question of Soviet immigration to Israel, for example, ambassadors to Arab countries, while defending Soviet policy as an integral part of domestic democratization, have joined with their Arab hosts in condemning the alleged settlement of these immigrants in the occupied territories. Alexander Zotov was quoted on Syrian Radio as saying that Israeli policy was "a crude violation of international law and a blatant defiance of the UN," and Gennadi Zhurabelev, writing in *Al-Ahram*, accused Israel of exploiting the immigration to pressure the United States for more assistance and of settling Soviet Jews in the Territories in order to extract greater concessions from the Palestinians.[87] At the same time, the Soviet mission in Israel, almost certainly by Ministry directive, declined an invitation by Yitzhak Shamir to check for itself the extent of Soviet Jewish settlement in the Territories.[88] It may well be that information from the Foreign Ministry prompted Gorbachev, at the end of a summit meeting in the United States, to condemn so strongly the settlement of Soviet Jews in the Territories and even to hint that he might stop issuing exit permits if this activity did not cease.[89]

By contrast, many Soviet journalists, writing for a home audience, took a more restrained and informed position. A. Shumilin, for example, conceded the existence of a problem but was careful to note that only 1.5 percent of former Soviet citizens were living in the Territories.[90] And after a personal tour, the foreign editor of *Moskovskaya Novosti*, Sergei Velovich, expressed his opposition to any Jewish settlement in the Territories but conceded that among Soviet Jews, settlement in the Territories was a very limited phenomenon.[91] Speculation about an institutional bias is strengthened by the fact that, unlike the Soviet Foreign Ministry, several republics have shown no reluctance whatsoever in sending senior representatives to Israel to meet with their Israeli counterparts. Perhaps most revealing of all is the fact that economic delegations to Israel even came from the Muslim republics of Uzbekistan and Kazakhstan.[92]

Bureaucratic politics are not a new phenomenon in Soviet foreign policy; a role for public opinion in foreign policy would be. However the precise impact, if any, of public opinion is difficult to judge. In the broadest sense, it almost certainly militates against military intervention abroad. After Afghanistan, the Soviet Union experienced something like a "Vietnam syndrome." Some of its manifestations were diminishing prestige of the military in society, rising rates of draft-evasion and desertion, and general demoralization. Another consequence was a widespread aversion to involvement in hostilities abroad, and this factor, more than any diplomatic calculation, may well explain the refusal of the Soviet Union to participate in the military coalition against Iraq.[93] As one newspaper put it, "Haven't enough young men already died in Afghanistan, and aren't enough still dying in Armenia, Azerbaijan, Uzbekistan, and Kirgizia?"[94]

But while there may well be greater attention to public opinion on overarching issues such as foreign military intervention, the Soviet attitude toward parties in specific Middle Eastern conflicts seems not to be strongly correlated with the attitudes imputed to domestic constituencies or to government concerns about them. The most important domestic consideration in this context would seem to be the sensitivities of Soviet Muslims, who account for at least 20 percent of the population. Apart from a large concentration of Tartars in the Volga Valley, they live mostly, though not exclusively, in Azerbaijan and the five republics of Central Asia. As late as 1986, official dogma held that the "brilliant resolution of the nationality question in the USSR represents one of the greatest triumphs of socialism."[95] Nevertheless, Soviet authorities were becoming increasingly uneasy about the rising nationalism of the Muslim peoples, and more recent commentaries betray real fear and revulsion at the prospect of Islamic fundamentalism.

Since the Alma-Ata riots in December 1986, which were provoked by the appointment of an ethnic Russian as first secretary of the Kazakh Communist Party Central Committee, there have been violent disturbances in all of the Muslim republics, resulting in hundreds of deaths, large-scale property damage and the intimidation of non-local populations (especially Russian "settlers"); in January 1990, martial law was declared and large regular army forces were used to crush unrest in Azerbaijan. On many occasions, officials warned that outside incitement was exacerbating the problem, with Iran being a particular source of concern. One early example was the complaint by a Central Committee secretary of the Turkmenistan Communist Party that Iranian broadcasts were having an "extremely negative influence" on the population.[96] During the fighting in Azerbaijan, Soviet and Iranian media traded strong accusations, with Radio Tehran criticizing the "violent treatment of the people of Azerbaijan" and Radio Moscow in Persian warning against "unconsidered nationalist or religious appeals."[97] Contrasting these events with the Soviet response to manifestations of nationalism in the Baltic republics, Muslims elsewhere expressed the suspicion that Soviet behavior was attributable to an anti-Muslim prejudice.[98] And during the Gulf crisis in 1990-91, there were numerous pro-Saddam statements and demonstrations by Soviet Muslims, and even some reports of Soviet Muslims trying to volunteer their services to fight for Iraq.[99]

Soviet officials are undoubtedly concerned about the possible foreign ramifications of domestic developments and, conversely, about the domestic political consequences of Islamic solidarity with foreign forces. Following the fighting in Azerbaijan, for example, First Deputy Foreign Minister Vorontsov felt it necessary to meet with the heads of Arab diplomatic missions in Moscow in order to dispel the notion that there was "an underlying religious cause" to the situation in the Transcaucasus.[100]

Nevertheless, if the Soviet leadership really ascribed much

importance to domestic Muslim opinion, or if it genuinely feared that contact with the Muslim world or identification with Muslim causes abroad was contributing to the rising self-assertion of Muslim nationalities within the Soviet Union, it would logically have behaved in the Middle East along different, more traditional lines: it would have supported Iraq or at least refrained from aligning itself with the US-led coalition, avoided any rapprochement with Israel, continued to act through its own forces to prevent the replacement of a "progressive" government in Afghanistan by Islamic fundamentalist forces liable to inspire imitation across the border, and prevented, or at least channeled through tightly-controlled official filters (the "registered mullahs") all contacts between Soviet Muslims and Muslims elsewhere.[101]

Instead, it did precisely the opposite. The policy of supporting the campaign against Iraq was challenged but never abandoned, relations with Israel were gradually but systematically improved, the withdrawal from Afghanistan took place on schedule (although post-withdrawal assistance increased), and channels for Muslim contacts abroad were greatly expanded; in 1990, the government authorized the import of hundreds of thousands of Korans from Saudi Arabia, expedited visa and financial arrangements for 1,500 Muslims to make the hajj pilgrimage (no more than 50-60 per year had gone before), approved the foreign visits of dozens of Muslim delegations, and opened up very loosely-controlled border crossing points with Iran and even Turkey (whose cultural and economic influence with Soviet Muslims is stronger than Iran's).[102] In short, the domestic "Muslim factor" in public opinion does not appear to have been a major element impeding implementation of new political thinking in the Middle East, particularly vis-a-vis Israel.

This may be because Soviet officials do not believe that Soviet Muslims are intensely aware of or concerned about the Middle East, especially Israel and the Arabs. The primary manifestations of Muslim identity thus far have been national or cultural, rather than religious, and to the extent that Soviet Muslims have an external referent, it is Turkish, or perhaps Iranian for the Tajiks, but not Arab. Indeed, Soviet Muslims have not even demonstrated much solidarity among themselves. Much of the violence in the

Muslim republics (apart from Azerbaijan) has been directed against Russians and central control, but a great deal has also been directed at other Muslims. Nor is there much evidence of a drive for unity along religious lines. The strongest proponents of any overarching pan-Turkic or pan-Islamic structures are the Uzbeks who, as the most numerous in Central Asia, are the most likely to dominate such structures, and it is precisely for this reason that the other nationalities have shown so little enthusiasm. Soviet Muslims, as Muslims, may be abstractly sympathetic to the Palestinians (and to other Middle Eastern Muslims involved in conflicts with non-Muslims), but unless they are swept up by a wave of fundamentalist fervor, they will probably be no more energized by the Israel-Arab conflict than are Muslims in Turkey, Malaysia, or Senegal.

A second explanation may be that Soviet (Russian) leaders simply do not care about alienating Soviet Muslims, and might even be secretly pleased if separatist tendencies in Central Asia were to intensify. At present, these appear to be much less pronounced than in the Baltic republics, Moldavia, or even western Ukraine. Indeed, apart from the "Slavic heartland" (Russia, Ukraine, Byelorussia), it is only the Muslim republics that have supported Gorbachev's efforts to preserve the Union through restructuring. In the other predominantly Christian republics — Estonia, Latvia, Lithuania, Moldavia, Georgia and Armenia — constitutional reform has been rejected in favor of complete independence.[103] Furthermore, there is a school of thought among Russian nationalists that makes little distinction between the Third World beyond Soviet borders and the Third World within, and whatever degree of indifference to the dangers of secession currently exists, it would almost certainly change to active encouragement if the "Russia First" school of thought were ultimately to prevail and the strain of Great Russian nationalism represented by Solzhenitsyn became the new, new political thinking.

4. *Irrationality*

Israel may be an aberration for the Soviet Union, in the sense that Soviet policy may be strongly influenced by sentiment, meaning anti-Semitism. Such irrationality may well help explain the prolonged delay in renewing diplomatic ties, and, even more so, in the refusal to admit publicly that the decision to break ties (which runs counter to the traditional preference for universal relations, at least in formal terms) was a mistake. Senior Soviet officials realized quite early on that the break in relations had been ill-considered; in 1970 or 1971, Gromyko privately conceded that the decision had "probably" been an error.[104] But the refusal to acknowledge this publicly and draw the appropriate conclusion contrasts sharply with more momentous admissions of Soviet foolishness or even illegality on far more cardinal issues: the invasion of Czechoslovakia, the deployment of SS-20 missiles in Europe, the construction of the Krasnoyarsk phased-array radar, the invasion of Afghanistan (which the commander of ground forces claimed was opposed by the military), even the 1940 murder of Polish officers at Katyn forest.[105]

In the face of such admissions, the Soviet insistence on making an exception on the issue of diplomatic relations and linking them to some concession by Israel suggests an element of malice and strengthens the suspicion voiced by a senior Soviet journalist that it is Russian anti-Semitism that is the obstacle to renewed ties.[106] It is immaterial whether this malice stems from ideological resentment of the fact that Jews, in sustaining their separate identity, disproved the thesis of the "new Soviet man," from an unsettled historical account with Zionists who fought communists for the loyalty of Jews before and after the Revolution, or simply from deep-seated Russian tradition. Anti-Semitism undeniably exists and somehow colors attitudes toward Israel, even if it does not fully determine policy outcomes. As one Soviet analyst suggests, it is "part of the overall context in which the official approach to the Middle Eastern problem is planned and implemented."[107]

Ironically, however, anti-Semitism may in some respects actually have helped accelerate the implementation of new thinking vis-a-vis Israel rather than retarding it. The stereotypical belief that Israel and world Jewry control western banks and mass media, to which the Soviets would dearly like access, would be an additional reason to cultivate Israeli goodwill. Anti-Semites would also be happy to permit increased Jewish emigration, in the hope that the Soviet Union could thereby rid itself of undesirable elements.[108] On balance, then, an element of irrationality in Soviet policy toward Israel may well be present, but its effects are ambiguous.

5. *Reaction to American Provocations*

The last stage of the Iran-Iraq War was the most blatant example of Soviet policy deviating from the rules of new thinking in regional conflicts, i.e., of not refraining from trying to gain a competitive advantage at American expense. Soviet policy toward Iran betrayed a priority for consolidating relations with that country rather than promoting an end to the war. During these years, however, American policy was consciously and almost provocatively motivated by the desire to exclude or contain Soviet presence. The "arms-for-hostages" deal, as has already been pointed out, was inspired by the perceived threat of Soviet penetration of Iran after the demise of Khomeini; the invitation to reflag Kuwaiti tankers, already under consideration but without any sense of urgency, was quickly accepted after it was learned that the Soviet Union had approved a similar Kuwaiti request, and the United States then refused to "share" the Kuwaiti tanker fleet with the Soviets, insisting instead that all 11 ships be given American registration.[109] Furthermore, the United States rebuffed every Soviet proposal to guarantee freedom of navigation through a multinational, UN-sponsored naval force. Instead, it persisted in excluding any Soviet naval presence because the prevailing attitude, as described by one former high American official, was "It's our Gulf."[110] There is nothing in the principles of new political thinking that requires reciprocity. In theory, the Soviet Union could implement any of them unilaterally and still achieve many of the desired results. However, any country, and especially one which still had pretensions at superpower status, would have found it difficult to resist the impulse to try to "get even."

6. *New Political Thinking is Hard to Recognize*

There is no obvious standard for judging what the unqualified implementation of new political thinking would produce. Logic suggests, however, that even the total transformation of the Soviet

Union into a democratic, non-expansionist, non-ideological state, devoid of any aspiration to engage in a zero-sum competition with the United States or "world imperialism" for global presence and influence — would still not renounce all the aspects of Soviet policy that may appear to contradict the principles, logic, or spirit of new political thinking.

Even a fully-transformed Soviet Union might, if it were still capable, intervene in regional conflicts, as France has done in Chad. Even such a Soviet Union might be interested in promoting its culture and language throughout the world, as France does. Even a Soviet Union guided by no vision other than the desire to improve foreign currency balances and domestic employment figures might continue to sell arms, without any paralyzing inhibitions about their possible impact on regional stability, democracy, or the wellbeing of customers' citizens or neighbors, as a long list of other countries do; Iraq's military buildup benefited immensely from Soviet assistance, but other countries, including the United States, also made major contributions.[111] Finally, even such a Soviet Union might be sensitive enough about national pride, prestige and independence to reject the appearance of being a subservient handmaiden or junior partner to the United States.

As the precedent of other retreating empires indicates, it is always difficult to adjust to a diminished international stature, and even if the Soviet Union is no longer able or willing to be a superpower, it will still want to look like a superpower, an equal partner, and will consciously distance itself, if only to a slight degree, from American policies on international affairs, whatever the merits of those policies might be. Thus, when Primakov was asked whether President Gorbachev had secured American agreement for his late-February proposals to end the war, he answered that this had not been necessary because "the Soviet Union has not been reduced to the status of a secondary power."[112]

Because of what has been called "the delusion...that it is the duty of a genuinely reformist Soviet Union to further the objectives of U.S. foreign policy,"[113] Soviet actions during the Gulf crisis led some American officials and analysts to wonder whether new political thinking was in retreat. Soviet mediation efforts were certainly not appreciated in the United States. But neither were those of France. Indeed, in many western countries, domestic debate about policy in the Gulf often revolved around the question, not of whether or not it was right, but of whether or not it was "dictated" by Washington. In short, it is possible that some of the shortcomings or inconsistencies in Soviet new thinking in the Middle East are really not shortcomings or inconsistencies at all, but rather represent the limits beyond which no major power, whatever its political thinking, is likely to go.

Apart from the first, these explanations, either separately or together in varying degrees, account for most of the partial, inconsistent or contradictory applications of new thinking in the Middle East. But apart from the first, none of them refutes the assessment that a change of historic proportions has taken place in Soviet behavior in the region, because of an even more profound change in the Soviet view of the importance of the Middle East (and the rest of the Third World) to its own security and other vital interests. The possible implications of these changes will be explored in the final chapter.

Chapter 5. Conclusions

For much of the Cold War period, Soviet relations with the communist states of Eastern Europe rested on a reliable system of controls: compliant local parties, infiltration of domestic security services, contrived economic dependency, and, in the last resort, the threat or use of the Red Army. No such mechanisms existed to control Soviet allies in the Third World. Instead, the relationship was more in the nature of a bargain: Soviet economic, military, and political support for local allies against their domestic or regional adversaries, in exchange for ideological and political support for the Soviet Union against its prime adversary — American-led imperialism. Soviet interest in gaining Third World support diminished when the Soviet leadership itself grew skeptical about the validity of the ideology and began to question the nature and purpose of the rivalry with the United States.

The result was declining interest in providing support to the Third World, that is, in the traditional bargain with Third World regimes. The shift does not stem from a different view of the intrinsic importance of the Third World or from changing priorities. Third World policy was always derivative of and subordinate to policy vis-a-vis the West, and it remained so in the era of new thinking. What changed was the Soviet view of the relationship with the West itself — from primarily competitive to primarily cooperative — and from this change, the perception of the diminishing value of the bargain with Third World regimes flowed almost automatically.

In the past, global considerations dictated great Soviet sensitivity to the local or regional concerns of the regimes it had "adopted" or wanted to cultivate. As applied in the Middle East, this meant that "...the lower the degree of Soviet control, the more wholeheartedly the USSR must identify itself with its clients' position in the Arab-Israeli conflict...."[1] Under Gorbachev, there has been no increase in control. But there has been a demonstrated willingness to put some distance between Soviet policy and Arab preferences on direct Arab-Israeli issues, such as UN votes or Jewish emigration, as well as on arms transfer questions, such as chemical weapons or missile proliferation. The latter are generally viewed by Arabs through the prism of the Arab-Israeli or other regional conflicts, but for the Soviet Union they constitute world order problems, that is, issues in their relations with the West.

At the 1989 chemical weapons conference in Paris, Soviet Deputy Foreign Minister Viktor Karpov was quite blunt in opposing the Arab demand to link chemical and nuclear disarmament, and in a secret document allegedly sent to the Arab League in 1990, the Soviet Union is reported to have pressured the Arabs to abandon their own position on this question.[2] Similarly, the Soviets' growing reluctance to provide all the surface-to-surface missiles requested by their Arab clients may well be due to obligations assumed under the terms of the 1987 INF Treaty and to the general Soviet desire to cooperate with the leading western countries on this issue; the Soviet Union did not formally join the Missile Technology Control Regime, but a joint communique issued at the end of the Baker-Shevardnadze meeting in Moscow in early 1990 stated that both countries were "observing the guiding principles of exports within the framework of the existing regime regarding missiles...."[3]

These incidents illustrate a relatively new Soviet determination to go beyond temporary collaboration in crisis management and to forge a more durable cooperative relationship with the United States, even at the risk of alienating Arab allies and losing position in the Middle East. In simple terms, presence and influence in the Middle East (and elsewhere in the Third World) are no longer seen as instrumentally useful in the relationship with the United States or as justifying Soviet commitments. And as long as this view persists, there is a far, far lower risk that a Middle Eastern war will have wider ramifications in the sense of triggering the mechanism that often produced Soviet-American crises. The escalation scenario that once caused so much extra-regional anxiety about regional conflicts is no longer plausible.

There is, however, less certainty about how Soviet new political thinking might affect the region itself. International terrorism is one area in which the impact may be felt. For many years, the Soviet Union and several communist regimes in Eastern Europe, especially East Germany and Bulgaria, provided considerable financial, logistical and training support for terrorist organizations which seemed hostile to western interests of one sort or another. Among these organizations were Arab and Iranian groups, including several factions of the PLO.[4] East Germany has ceased to exist and the other European former members of the Soviet bloc apparently intend to abandon their activities in this area. If terrorist organizations are also deprived of training facilities, safe houses, tactical advice, funds, weapons, documentation and other forms of support from Soviet sources, as new thinking indicates they will be, that cannot but undermine their effectiveness. At the same time, the Soviet bloc was never the sole, or even the most important source of state support for Middle Eastern terrorists. Most of these organizations have additional or alternative state sponsors within the Middle East itself, and unless those sponsors are also willing to withdraw their support, the direct impact of new political thinking on international terrorism will probably be less than decisive.

On other issues, the likely effect of new thinking is even less clear. The implications for the frequency and character of Middle Eastern wars are highly ambiguous. Even when it tried, the Soviet Union at the height of its influence could not always dissuade clients who were determined to initiate hostilities. It may be, however, that local clients were not dissuaded precisely because they believed that, regardless of formal positions, the dynamics of the Soviet-American competition would compel the Soviet Union to provide support in extremis and that they would certainly preclude Soviet sanctions. To the extent that this assumption played any role in the decisionmaking of regional powers, it is no longer sustainable, especially in the aftermath of the Iraqi invasion of Kuwait. This should logically reduce the likelihood of regional wars.

However, the prospect of active Soviet assistance was probably never a decisive factor, except insofar as it was needed to deter or frustrate anticipated American intervention (which Saddam Hussein was apparently convinced would not take place if he acted against Kuwait). In most cases, political needs and assessments of *local* military balances almost certainly played a weightier role. The first was normally unconnected to Soviet policy, but the second was definitely influenced by Soviet arms transfers, much more than by direct involvement. According to Alvin Rubinstein, "With the exception of the Indo-Pakistan wars in 1965 and 1971, every major local war between Third World protagonists was started by a Soviet-armed state."[5] Even if there were other exceptions to this generalization, there does appear to be a correlation between Soviet arms and the militarization of politics, because the regimes most closely associated with the Soviet Union tended to espouse more radical ideologies and to pursue revisionist policies.

In recent years, Soviet leaders have expressed increasing concern about the proliferation of nonconventional weapons and long-range delivery systems, especially ballistic missiles, in the Third World; apart from their general effect on regional stability, such weapons in the Middle East potentially pose a direct threat to Soviet security. In fact, the Soviet Union has consistently withheld both weapons of mass destruction and technologies that would facilitate their local production. On the other hand, it has been the most active proliferator of surface-to-surface missiles. Soviet missiles, especially the FROG-7 and Scud-B, are the most widespread in Middle Eastern arsenals; of the 10 regional states (including Kuwait) that possess surface-to-surface missiles, eight have Soviet models and a ninth, Iran, has received Scuds from other sources. New thinking will almost certainly sustain the refusal to sell nonconventional weapons and minimize or completely eliminate the willingness to transfer even those missile technologies formally permitted by international arms control agreements. It will also make the Soviet Union an active proponent of regional arms control agreements in these areas.[6]

If the Soviets were to undertake a similarly restrictive approach to conventional arms transfers, they could certainly exercise a restraining influence on regional arms races, hence, on the prospects that their traditional clients might pursue political objectives by military means. However, it is not at all clear that such a policy logically derives from new thinking or that it is likely to be adopted. If Soviet Third World policy is stripped of any ideological or imperial impulse, conventional arms transfers may decline slightly as grant aid and credit are further reduced, but those most sharply affected will be the poorest Soviet clients in Asia, Africa and Latin America. In the Middle East, a basically commercial policy will probably result in no substantial reductions except those stemming from the demand side. Indeed, Soviet exporters may aggressively search for new clients, including even Israel.[7] Following the Iraqi invasion of Kuwait, there were calls in the Soviet media for a reassessment even of commercial arms sales. The diplomatic correspondent of *Izvestia* observed, with an undertone of contrition, that the Soviet Union had turned Iraq into the most destabilizing force in the region, and the weekly *Novaya Vremya* asked Deputy Foreign Minister Belonogov if the Iraqi action did not indicate that much more caution should be exercised in selling arms to "friendly states."[8]

But barring the creation of a truly effective international regime that will somehow regulate the global arms trade, it is unlikely that the Soviet Union will unilaterally restrain itself for political, strategic, or moral reasons and thereby lose its share of the market to other suppliers — the United States, mid-size powers like Britain, France, and China, or emerging producers like Brazil, Argentina, and North Korea, for whom non-economic considerations are virtually non-existent. Soviet arms sales will probably be viewed as a matter of economic necessity; conversion is not easy, the Soviets are far less competitive in other fields, and they already have an established semi-captive market (at least in the short term). Moreover, the power of inertia cannot be underestimated. Even the post-communist government of Czechoslovakia, which is much more categorically distinguished from its immediate predecessor, has discovered that inherited contracts and disproportionate dependence on arms exports for foreign currency make it impossible to sever business dealings abruptly, even in the most unsavory of commodities (such as Semtex) and with the most disreputable of customers.[9]

Whatever the impact of changes in Soviet policy and the nature of the superpower relationship on the probability or frequency of war, they are likely to have a significant impact on the character of wars that do break out. If new thinking removes Middle Eastern conflicts from the Soviet-American agenda, there will be no strong superpower commitments to regional belligerents, hence, less urgency in preventing certain developments in regional wars that could have caused a superpower confrontation. A reduced incentive to intervene may permit these wars to be fought to a decisive conclusion, resulting in far greater political convulsions than has been the case in most Israeli-Arab wars since 1948. Alternatively, greater superpower disinterest in war-termination measures may permit local wars between evenly matched adversaries to go on indefinitely. In some respects, the eight-year Iran-Iraq War was a precursor of this trend, but the protracted civil wars in Lebanon, and even more so in Sudan, constitute particularly instructive paradigms.

Similar ambiguity attaches to question of peace and the prospects for effective conflict resolution measures by the superpowers. Within the framework of new thinking, the Soviet interest in the settlement of these conflicts, particularly the Arab-Israel conflict, should be self-evident. Aside from the natural apprehension of any state about violent instability in areas close to its own borders, the Soviets are instinctively averse to an American military presence nearby (which is required or facilitated by regional conflicts), regardless of how marginal it may be in terms of the overall Soviet-American military balance or of the practical threat it may pose.[10] The Soviets may also fear that active conflicts will strengthen the Islamic tendency in various Middle Eastern states and that this, in turn, will lead to emulation, if not active subversion, in their own Muslim areas. Finally, the spread of weapons of mass destruction and long-range delivery systems in the Middle East means that the outbreak of a war in the area may lead to collateral damage against the Soviet Union itself. All these considerations indicate that the expressed Soviet preference for a peaceful resolution of conflicts in the Middle East is genuine; the last explains the particularly strong Soviet emphasis on arms control, frequently to the point where it almost appears to be a substitute for political agreements among Middle Eastern belligerents.

At the same time, it is objectively difficult for the Soviet Union to make a major active contribution to conflict resolution: it has few "reassurance" assets to offer, and its coercive capabilities, despite occasional hints that its role is to bring its Arab partners to the table, were not even sufficient to bring Syria to the 1973 Geneva Conference, which the Soviet Union itself endorsed and participated in when Syria was at the peak of its vulnerability and dependency. Despite the Soviet desire to be seen as an equal partner in the Arab-Israeli peace process, it is not clear what assets the Soviet Union can bring to bear on that process. In any event, the ability of recalcitrant regional actors to defy superpower allies, especially the Soviet Union, should not be underestimated. As a result, many of the highly-publicized successes of Soviet-American cooperation in regional conflicts since 1985 have actually been successes only at superpower disengagement. Conflicts in Afghanistan, Cambodia, Ethiopia, Chad and Angola were not all resolved; in several cases, the war simply continued without direct superpower involvement.

It is not inconceivable that some combination of Soviet passivity and American activism might help animate the Arab-Israeli peace process. Deprived of Soviet military, economic and diplomatic support, the most radical Arab protagonists (i.e., precisely those most dependent on Soviet help in the past) may well despair of ever achieving their most ambitious objectives and resign themselves, however grudgingly, to more modest terms; this was almost certainly the decisive factor in Syrian President Hafiz al-Asad's decision in July 1991 to accept the American proposal for a peace conference which essentially entailed direct negotiations with Israel. By the same token, the United States, no longer preoccupied with the global ramifications of pressure on an established ally, may act more aggressively to persuade Israel to compromise on its demands, as well. If so, there should logically be a greater chance of reaching common ground.

On the other hand, with less concern on the part of both superpowers about the likely consequences of stalemate — damage to an ally, defection of an ally, eruption of war and the possible need for superpower involvement — there may also be less compulsion to break the stalemate by actively promoting a peace settlement, and assuming the costs and obligations that would inevitably entail.

The systematic consolidation of stable, cooperative relations with the West, which began in 1985 as a corollary of the economic need to restructure, had become by 1990 an existential imperative. A breakdown of the distribution system had brought the Soviet Union, if not to the brink of famine, at least to its most difficult winter since World War II; the same country which bought wheat from the United States in the 1970s was now receiving charity packages from Germany (including food stores once stockpiled in Berlin against the danger of a Soviet blockade). There were also strong secessionist movements in every Union Republic, including Russia itself. The concerns expressed since 1985 that Gorbachev, democratization, new political thinking, or even the Soviet Union itself might not survive were informed by a new sense of immediacy. Nevertheless, there was simply no reliable instrument for predicting developments in domestic Soviet politics, and therefore little point in trying.

But even if the most radical reversals of course took place, and the craving for domestic order and discipline resulted in the restoration of the ancien regime (pre-1985 or pre-1917), there was no intrinsic reason for the Soviet Union to reverse course in the Middle East, or elsewhere in the Third World. Without underestimating the importance of personality or ideology, the analysis of Soviet interests that eventuated in new thinking on regional conflicts nevertheless remained valid. To secure its direct material interests in the Middle East (access to regional markets and resources), the Soviet Union needed merely to act like a normal international power; only pride and prestige recommended intense political/security involvement and the assumption of commitments inherent in anything other than a largely symbolic regional role. This appears to be the operational meaning of new Soviet political thinking in the Middle East, and its logic has been acknowledged, explicitly or implicitly, for several years. Simply put, the Soviet Union had little to show for the massive investment and considerable risks it had run in the region; the region, like the rest of the Third World, contributed little to the struggle against imperialism, and the point of that struggle itself became increasingly dubious. In the reportage of a 1988 symposium in Amman on Soviet-Arab relations, for example, the Soviet side stressed the many advantages to the Arabs of Soviet-Arab cooperation but neither side could point out a single Soviet benefit.[11] And there is no reason to assume that this logic will cease to be persuasive to Soviet publics and leaders after Gorbachev leaves the scene.

As for the Middle East itself, the effect of new thinking depends on how far its principles are pushed, not only in the Soviet Union, but elsewhere as well. In the unlikely event that it is taken to its logical extreme and adopted universally, new political thinking may produce some world order that proceeds even beyond the collective security envisaged (or hoped for) by the framers of the United Nations Charter to encompass active conflict resolution. Otherwise, the impact on the prospects for war and peace in the Middle East will almost certainly be positive, but Soviet policy alone hardly guarantees a revolutionary change. After all, new political thinking has helped to eliminate regional conflicts in other parts of the world as potential causes of superpower confrontation; but despite undeniable efforts to resolve those conflicts, the fighting often goes on.

For Israel, the most profound consequence of changes in Soviet policy is the massive Jewish immigration which, in its numbers and talents, constitutes a source of potentially tremendous strength. In other respects, the Soviet Union, either in its present configuration or as a reconstituted Russia, may play a more constructive role in the region, but the most important foreign power for Israel and for the rest of the Middle East will remain, as always, the United States. In the last analysis, however, the key to the future for all people in the Middle East rests, as always, in their own hands.

APPENDIX

Fundamental Principles of International Security

1. In the military sphere
   i. renunciation by the nuclear powers of war — both nuclear and conventional — against each other or against third countries;
   ii. prevention of an arms race in outer space, cessation of all nuclear weapons tests and the total destruction of such weapons, a ban on the destruction [sic] of chemical weapons, and renunciation of the development of other means of mass annihilation;
   iii. a strictly controlled lowering of the levels of military capabilities of countries to limits of reasonable sufficiency;
   iv. disbandment of military alliances, and, as a stage toward this, renunciation of their enlargement and of the formation of new ones;
   v. balanced and proportionate reduction of military budgets.

2. In the political sphere
   i. strict respect in international practice for the right of each people to choose the ways and forms of its development independently;
   ii. a just political settlement of international crises and regional conflicts;
   iii. elaboration of a set of measures aimed at building confidence between states and the creation of effective guarantees against attack from without and for inviolability of their frontiers;
   iv. elaboration of effective methods of preventing international terrorism, including those ensuring the safety of international land, air and sea communications.

3. In the economic sphere
   i. exclusion of all forms of discrimination from internation-

al practice; renunciation of the policy of economic blockades and sanctions if this is not directly envisaged in the recommendations of the world community;

ii. joint quests for ways of a just settlement of the problem of debts;
iii. establishment of a new world economic order guaranteeing equal economic security to all countries;
iv. elaboration of principles for utilizing part of the funds released as a result of reduction of military budgets for the good of the world community, of developing nations in the first place;
v. the pooling of efforts in exploring and making peaceful use of outer space and in resolving global problems on which the destinies of civilization depend.

4. In the humanitarian sphere

i. cooperation in the dissemination of the ideas of peace, disarmament, and international security; greater flow of general objective information and broader contact between peoples for the purpose of learning about one another; reinforcement of the spirit of mutual understanding and concord in relations between them;
ii. extirpation of genocide, apartheid, advocacy of fascism and every other form of racial, national or religious exclusiveness, and also of discrimination against people on this basis;
iii. extension — while respecting the laws of each country — of international cooperation in the implementation of the political, social and personal rights of people;
iv. solution in a humane and positive spirit to questions related to the reuniting of families, marriage, and the promotion of contacts between people and between organizations;
v. strengthening of and the quests for new forms of cooperation in culture, art, science, education, and medicine.

SOURCE: Mikhail Gorbachev, *Perestroika: New Thinking for Our Country and The World* (London: Collins, 1987), p. 231.

Notes

Chapter 1

[1] Cited in Alfred Meyer, *Leninism* (Cambridge, Mass.: Harvard University Press, 1957), p. 241.
[2] *Imperialism: The Highest Stage of Capitalism* (Peking, 1969), p. 9.
[3] Francis Fukuyama, for example, discerns ten phases of Soviet policy since the Revolution, each (with one exception) defined as "an alternating cycle of left- and right-wing strategies." "Patterns of Soviet Third World Policy," *Problems of Communism* 36, no. 5 (September-October 1987), p. 5.
[4] *Critical Remarks on the National Question* (Moscow: 1960), p. 185.
[5] Quoted in Jane Degras (ed.), *The Communist International, 1919-1943: Documents*, Vol. I (London, 1956), p. 144.
[6] Degras, *The Communist International*, p. 390.
[7] *Marxism and the National and Colonial Question* (London: n.d.), p. 193.
[8] Curt Gasteyger, "The Soviet Union and the Tiers Monde," *Survey*, no. 43 (August 1962), p. 341.
[9] Rajan Menon, *Soviet Power in the Third World* (New Delhi: East-West Press, 1989), p. 1.
[10] Donald S. Carlisle, "Stalin's Postwar Foreign Policy and the National Liberation Movements," *The Review of Politics* 27, no. 4 (July 1965), p. 341.
[11] Carlisle, "Stalin's Postwar Policy," p. 356; Fukuyama, "Patterns of Soviet Third World Policy," p. 3.
[12] Donald S. Carlisle, "The Changing Soviet Perception of the Development Process in the Afro-Asian World," *Midwest Journal of Political Science* 8, no. 4 (November 1964), p. 391.
[13] O.V. Kuusinen et al., *Fundamentals of Marxism-Leninism*, second edition (Moscow, 1963), pp. 421-22.
[14] Cited in BBC, *Summary of World Broadcasts* (henceforth, SWB), ME/3380/A/5 (16 May 1970).
[15] "Patterns of Soviet Policy," p. 4; see also Alvin Z. Rubinstein, *Moscow's Third World Strategy* (Princeton, 1988), pp. 51-64.
[16] Neil MacFarlane, "The USSR and the Third World: Continuity and Change under Gorbachev," *Harriman Institute Forum* 1, no. 3 (March 1988), pp. 1-2.
[17] Menon, *Soviet Power and the Third World*, pp. 173-74.

Abraham S. Becker places total military grants *and* sales during this period at about $500 million per annum. See "The Soviet Union and the Third World: The Economic Dimension," in Andrzej Korbonski and Francis Fukuyama (eds.), *The Soviet Union and the Third World: The Last Three Decades* (Ithaca & London: Cornell University Press, 1987), pp. 69, 78-79. According to Mark N. Kramer, economic assistance averaged $425 million annually, some $50 million more than average military aid. "Note: Soviet Arms Transfers to the Third World," *Problems of Communism* 36, no. 5 (September-October 1987), p. 53.

[18] Computed from Kramer, "Soviet Arms Transfers," pp. 53-55, and Becker, "The Economic Dimension," pp. 78-79. The latter source claims that agreements during this decade may have reached $5 billion per annum.

[19] Jerry F. Hough, "The End of Russia's 'Khomeini' Period: Dilemmas for U.S. Foreign Policy," *World Policy Journal* 4, no. 4 (Fall 1987), pp. 583-604.

[20] Computed from Becker, "The Economic Dimension," pp. 70, 78-79.

[21] Kramer, "Soviet Arms Transfers," pp. 61-62.

[22] For more on the conditions facilitating Soviet interventionism in these years, see MacFarlane, "The USSR and the Third World," pp. 2-3; Menon, *Soviet Power and the Third World*, pp. 89-166; and Rubinstein, *Moscow's Third World Strategy*, pp. 160-62.

[23] Francis Fukuyama, "Soviet Strategy in the Third World," in Korbonski and Fukuyama, *The Soviet Union and the Third World*, pp. 24-45.

[24] Charles Wolf, Jr., et al., *The Costs of the Soviet Empire*, R-3073/1-NA (Santa Monica: RAND Corporation, 1983), cited in Becker, "The Economic Dimension," pp. 90-91, and Menon, *Soviet Power and the Third World* p. 158.

Chapter 2

[1] Paul B. Henze, "The Russians and Arabia: Marginal Success," in Alexandre Bennigsen et al., *Soviet Strategy and Islam* (Basingstoke: Macmillan, 1989), p. 101.
[2] Quoted in Robert E. Hunter, *The Soviet Dilemma in the Middle East. Part I: The Problem of Commitment*, Adelphi Paper no. 59 (London: Institute for Strategic Studies, September 1969), p. 5.
[3] *Khrushchev Remembers*, translated and edited by Strobe Talbott (Boston: Little, Brown, 1970), p. 431.
[4] Quoted in N.H. Mager and Jacques Katel (eds.), *Conquest Without War* (New York: Simon and Schuster, 1961), p. 134.
[5] Alexander J. Bennett, "Arms Transfer as an Instrument of Soviet Policy in the Middle East," *Middle East Journal* 39, no. 4 (Autumn 1985), pp. 761-62.
[6] Abraham S. Becker, "A Note on Soviet Arms Transfers to the Middle East," in Steven L. Spiegel, Mark A. Heller, and Jacob Goldberg (eds.), *The Soviet-American Competition in the Middle East* (Lexington: Lexington Books, 1988), p. 55.
[7] Becker, "A Note," p. 55, and "The Economic Dimension," p. 72.
[8] Figures taken from Becker, "The Economic Dimension," pp. 75, 79.
[9] Gur Ofer and Joseph Pelzman, "Soviet Economic Interests in the Middle East," in Spiegel et al., *The Soviet-American Competition*, p. 234.
[10] The figure for the Egyptian debt is taken from Galia Golan, "Gorbachev's Middle East Strategy," *Foreign Affairs* 66, no. 1 (Fall 1987), p. 49. John P. Hannah estimates the Syrian military debt at $9-20 billion, in *At Arms Length: Soviet-Syrian Relations in the Gorbachev Era*. Policy Paper no. 18. (Washington, DC: The Washington Institute for Near East Policy, 1989), p. 33. According to another source, total Syrian indebtedness to Soviet-bloc nations, most of it to the Soviet Union, came to $15 billion in 1988. James Hansen, "Moscow and Damascus: How Binding the Ties?" *International Defense Review*, no. 8 (August 1988), p. 927. In early 1990, *Literaturnaya Gazeta* put the figure for the two countries at $4.5 billion and $12 billion, respectively. *U.S.S.R. Monitor* (Washington: The Heritage Foundation), no. 7 (February 1990).
[11] *Khrushchev Remembers*, p. 440.
[12] The architect of the Soviet global naval strategy and the "blue-water" navy, Admiral Sergei Gorshkov, has sometimes been compared to Admiral Alfred Mahan, the "father" of modern American naval thinking. During the 75 years that separated Mahan and Gorshkov, however, a great deal had happened, including the development of invulnerable long-range nuclear delivery vehicles.
[13] Anwar el-Sadat, *In Search of Identity: An Autobiography* (New York: Harper & Row, 1977), p. 231. See, also, Mohamed Heikal, *The Road to Ramadan* (New York: Ballantine, 1975), pp. 180-82.
[14] Robert O. Freedman, "Soviet Policy Toward Syria Since Camp

David," *Middle East Review* 14, nos. 1-2 (Fall-Winter 1981/82), p. 36.

[15] I. William Zartman, "The Strategy of Preventive Diplomacy in Third World Conflicts," in Alexander L. George, *Managing U.S.-Soviet Rivalry: Problems of Crisis Prevention* (Boulder, CO: Westview Press, 1983), p. 362.

[16] Rajan Menon, *Soviet Power and the Third World* (New Delhi: East-West Press, 1989), p. 235.

[17] The ability of small states to manipulate large patrons, despite huge disparities in measurable power, is analyzed, inter alia, in Robert Keohane, "The Big Influence of Small Allies," *Foreign Policy*, no. 2 (Spring 1971), pp. 161-82; Robert L. Rothstein, *The Weak in the World of the Strong* (New York: Columbia University Press, 1977), pp. 119-247; and Michael I. Handel, "Does the Dog Wag the Tail or Vice Versa? Patron-Client Relations," *Jerusalem Journal of International Relations* 6, no. 2 (1982), pp. 24-35.

[18] Glenn H. Snyder and Paul Diesing, *Conflict Among Nations: Bargaining, Decision-Making, and System Structure in International Crises* (Princeton: Princeton University Press, 1977), pp. 441-42.

[19] *Aviation Week and Space Technology*, May 18, 1970.

[20] Itamar Rabinovich and Asher Susser, "Mutual Encroachment: The United States and the Soviet Union in Syria and Jordan," in Spiegel et al., *The Soviet-American Competition in the Middle East*, p. 302.

[21] For a more detailed review of developments leading up to the intervention, see Mark A. Heller, "The Soviet Invasion of Afghanistan," *The Washington Quarterly* 3, no. 3 (Summer 1980), pp. 36-45.

[22] J. Bruce Amstutz, *Afghanistan: The First Five Years of Soviet Occupation* (Washington, DC: National Defense University Press, 1986), pp. 37-38.

[23] Steven R. David, "Africa: Moscow's Dubious Investment," *The National Interest*, no. 12 (Summer 1988), p. 135.

[24] Amstutz, *Afghanistan*, p. 255; Richard F. Grimmett, *Trends in Conventional Arms Transfers to the Third World by Major Supplier, 1982-1989*, Congressional Research Service Report 90-298F (Washington, DC: The Library of Congress, June 19, 1990), p. 60, Table 2J.

[25] For a more detailed treatment of the Egyptian-Iraqi rift and resulting Soviet embarrassments, see Nadav Safran, *From War to War: The Arab-Israeli Confrontation, 1948-1967* (New York: Pegasus, 1969), pp. 123-27; and Malcolm H. Kerr, *The Arab Cold War: Gamal Abd al-Nasir and His Rivals, 1958-1970*, third edition (London: Oxford University Press, 1971), pp. 16-21.

[26] The following account is largely based on Larry C. Napper, "The Ogaden War: Some Implications for Crisis Prevention," in George, *Managing U.S.-Soviet Rivalry*, pp. 223-53.

[27] The following analysis is largely based on Mark A. Heller, *The Iran-Iraq War: Implications for Third Parties* (Tel Aviv and Cambridge: Jaffee Center for Strategic Studies and Harvard Center

for International Affairs, 1984), pp. 32-35, and "Soviet and American Attitudes Toward the Iran-Iraq War," in Spiegel et al., *The Soviet-American Competition*, pp. 270-77.

28 Becker, "The Economic Dimension," p. 78.

29 Shahram Chubin, "The USSR and Southwest Asia," in Korbonski and Fukuyama, *The Soviet Union and the Third World*, p. 158.

30 Yevgeny M. Primakov, "The Soviet Union's Interests: Myths and Reality," in *AEI Foreign Policy and Defense Review* 6, no. 1 (1986), p. 29.

31 Chubin, "Gains for Soviet Policy in the Middle East," *International Security* 6, no. 4 (Spring 1982), pp. 140-41.

32 Karen Dawisha, "Moscow and the Gulf War," *The World Today* (January 1981), pp. 11-12.

33 *Radio Monte Carlo*, cited in Foreign Broadcast Information Service, *Daily Report: Mideast and North Africa* (henceforth FBIS/NES), June 1, 1982, p. C2; Drew Middleton, "New Iraqi Strategy is Seen in War with Iran," *New York Times*, October 31, 1982.

34 *New York Times*, November 17, 1982.

35 Alexander L. George, "Crisis Prevention Reexamined," in George, *Managing U.S.-Soviet Rivalry*, pp. 381-82.

36 *Anatomy of the Middle East Conflict* (Moscow: Nauka Publishing House), pp. 6, 309-10.

37 For a high-ranking insider's testimony and criticism of political backing of "extreme Arab demands," see Arkady N. Shevchenko, *Breaking With Moscow* (New York: Ballantine, 1985), pp. 178-79, 345-46.

38 Cited in *Current Digest of the Soviet Press* 19, no. 39 (October 18, 1967), p. 15.

39 *Khrushchev Remembers*, p. 433.

40 Heikal, *The Road to Ramadan*, pp. 81-82.

41 According to Sadat, the first such representation came from the Soviet ambassador within six hours of the Egyptian attack. *In Search of Identity*, p. 252.

42 For more on this little-publicized incident, see Safran, *From War to War*, pp. 115-19.

43 Hansen, "Moscow and Damascus," p. 925; Hannah, *At Arms Length*, p. 26.

44 David A. Korn, "U.S.-Soviet Negotiations of 1969 and the Rogers Plan," *Middle East Journal* 44, no. 1 (Winter 1990), 37-50.

45 Heikal, *The Road to Ramadan*, p. 222. It could be argued, of course, that the Soviets hoped that Arab support for the deteriorating position of Egypt and Syria would spare them the need to intervene themselves.

46 According to Sadat's testimony, the Soviets habitually tried to set the Arab leaders "by the ears" and to provoke Abd al-Nasir by depicting the Syrian leadership as "more progressive." *In Search of Identity*, p. 172.

47 Safran, *From War to War*, p. 278.

48 *Khrushchev Remembers*, p. 450.

49 *New York Times*, June 22, 1967.

Chapter 3

1 Paul Marantz, *From Lenin to Gorbachev: Changing Soviet Perspectives on East-West Relations*, Occasional Paper no. 4 (Ottawa: Canadian Institute for International Peace and Security, May 1988), pp. 48-49; David W. Chodikoff, "Political Dimensions of Superpower Intervention in the Gulf," in R.B. Byers and David Leyton-Brown (eds.), *Superpower Intervention in the Persian Gulf*, Polaris Papers no. 2 (Toronto: Canadian Institute of Strategic Studies, 1982), p. 28.

2 Yaacov Ro'i, "A New Soviet Policy Towards Israel?" *The Jerusalem Quarterly*, no. 44 (Fall 1987), p. 7; Richard Herrmann, "Soviet Policy and the Arab-Israeli Conflict: Actions, Patterns and Interpretations," *Political Science Quarterly* 102, no. 3 (Fall 1987), pp. 417-18.

3 Menon, *Soviet Power and the Third World*, p. 155, citing CIA sources.

4 Abel Aganbegyan, "Acceleration and Perestroika," in Aganbegyan and Timor Timofeyev, *The New Stage of Perestroika* (New York: Institute for East-West Security Studies, 1988), pp. 27-28.

5 *Ibid.*, pp. 31-35.

6 Oleg T. Bogomolov, "The Origins of Change in the Soviet Union," in *The Strategic Implications of Change in the Soviet Union*, Adelphi Paper 247 (London: International Institute for Strategic Studies, Winter 1989/90), p. 16.

7 Aganbegyan, "Acceleration and Perestroika," pp. 28-31.

8 Mikhail Gorbachev, *Perestroika: New Thinking for Our Country and The World* (London: Collins, 1987), p. 34.

9 *Ibid.*, pp. 28-32.

10 See Graham E. Fuller, "The Case for Optimism," in "The Empire's New Clothes," *The National Interest*; and Stephen M. Meyer, "The Sources and Prospects of Gorbachev's New Thinking on Security," *International Security* 13, no. 2 (Fall 1988), p. 129.

11 *Ibid.*, p. 132.

12 *Ibid.*, *passim*. See, also Jack Snyder, "The Gorbachev Revolution: A Waning of Soviet Expansionism?" *International Security* 12, no. 3 (Winter 1987/88), pp. 93-131; Bogomolov, "The Origins of Change," pp. 27-28; and Robert Legvold, "The Revolution in Soviet Foreign Policy," *Foreign Affairs* 68, no. 1 (1989), pp. 84-87. A particularly detailed analysis of changes in military doctrine may be found in Meyer, "The Sources and Prospects of Gorbachev's New Political Thinking," pp. 124-163.

13 *Perestroika*, pp. 144-46, 221-22; Andrei V. Kozirev, "Regional Conflict: Cooperation and Competition," in *The Strategic Implications of Change in the Soviet Union*, Part II, Adelphi Paper 248 (London: International Institute for Strategic Studies, Winter 1989/90), p. 46.

14 *Perestroika*, p. 150.

15 Elizabeth Kridl Valkenier, "New Soviet Thinking About the Third World," *World Policy Journal* 4, no. 4 (Fall 1987), pp. 662-63.

[16] Henry Trofimenko, "The Third World and the US-Soviet Competition: A Soviet View," *Foreign Affairs* 59, no. 5 (Summer 1981), p. 1027.

[17] "East-West: Quest for New Relations. On the Priorities of the Soviet State's Foreign Policy," *Literaturnaya Gazeta*, in FBIS-SOV (May 20, 1988), p. 7. For additional examples of admissions that western reactions had been provoked by Soviet actions, see Stephen F. Larrabee, "Regional Conflict: Cooperation and Competition," in *The Strategic Implications of Change in the Soviet Union*, Part II, Adelphi Paper 248 (International Institute for Strategic Studies, Winter 1989/90), pp. 61-62.

[18] "Foreign Policy: Lessons of the Past," *International Affairs*, no. 6 (June 1989), p. 83.

[19] Igor Malashenko, "Ideals and Interests," *New Times*, no. 45 (November 1988), p. 28.

[20] See for example, David E. Albright, "The USSR and the Third World in the 1980's," *Problems of Communism* 38, nos. 2-3 (March-June 1989), p. 69.

[21] George Breslauer, "All Gorbachev's Men," in "The Empire's New Clothes: Moscow and the Third World After Afghanistan," *The National Interest*, no. 12 (Summer 1988), p. 92.

[22] Snyder, "The Gorbachev Revolution," p. 117.

[23] Hough, "The End of Russia's 'Khomeini' Period," p. 592.

[24] Dashichev, "East-West," p. 8. See also Walter Laqueur, "Glasnost Abroad: New Thinking in Foreign Policy," *The Washington Quarterly* 11, no. 4 (Autumn 1988), pp. 77-78.

[25] For more details, see S. Neil MacFarlane, "The Soviet Union and Southern African Security," *Problems of Communism* 38, nos. 2-3 (March-June 1989), pp. 82-84; and *The Washington Post*, June 3, 1989.

[26] Larrabee, "Regional Conflict," pp. 64-65; *Economist Foreign Report* (December 7, 1989), p. 8.

[27] Rajan Menon, "New Thinking and Northeast Asian Security," *Problems of Communism* 38, nos. 2-3 (March-June 1989), pp. 11-12, 15-16; *International Herald Tribune*, January 16, 1990.

[28] Ilya Prizel, "Latin America: The Long March," in "The Empire's New Clothes," p. 117.

[29] Valkenier, "New Soviet Thinking," p. 653.

[30] Quoted in Francis Fukuyama, *Gorbachev and the New Soviet Agenda in the Third World*, R-3634-A (Santa Monica: Rand Corporation (June 1989), p. 10.

[31] Valkenier, "New Soviet Thinking," p. 659.

[32] Menon, "New Thinking and Northwest Asian Security," pp. 24-26.

[33] *Washington Post*, December 16, 1989.

[34] For example, deliveries of supersonic combat aircraft fell from 1340 in 1982-85 to 615 in 1986-89. Grimmett, *Trends in Conventional Arms Transfers*, p. 72. The value of agreements was almost $25 billion in 1984 and $11.2 billion in 1989 (p. 13). Numbers of weapons delivered are shown in Table 3, p. 66.

[35] *Soviet Military Power 1990* (Washington: United States Government Printing Office, 1990), p. 18.

[36] See in particular Valkenier, "New Soviet Thinking About the Third World," pp. 654-58; and Fukuyama, *Gorbachev and the New Soviet Agenda*, pp. 15-17.
[37] Menon, *Soviet Power and the Third World*, p. 59.
[38] Albright, "The USSR and the Third World," p. 57; Celeste A. Wallander, "Third World Conflict in Soviet Military Thought: Does the 'New Thinking' Grow Prematurely Grey?" *World Politics* 42, no. 1 (October 1989), p. 36.
[39] MacFarlane, "The Soviet Union and Southern African Security," p. 84.
[40] International Institute for Strategic Studies, *The Military Balance* (London: 1981-82 through 1990-91).
[41] Zalmay Khalilzad, "Afghanistan: Anatomy of a Soviet Failure," in "The Empire's New Clothes," pp. 25-26.
[42] MacFarlane, "The USSR and the Third World," p. 5, and "The Soviet Union and Southern African Security," pp. 85-87; and Rubinstein, *Moscow's Third World Strategy*, p. 288.
[43] All figures in current dollars, taken from Grimmett, *Trends in Conventional Arms Transfers*, pp. 59-61.
[44] There was additional evidence of serious strains in Soviet-Cuban relations in 1989, including scathing attacks by Castro on political reforms in Eastern Europe and a ban on the distribution in Cuba of excessively liberal Soviet publications such as *Moscow News* and *Sputnik*. Margot Light, "Soviet Policy in the Third World," *International Affairs* 67, no. 2 (April 1991), p. 275.
[45] Figures from Larrabee, "Regional Conflict," p. 59; Charles Krauthammer, "Soviet Empire: A Paradoxical Collapse," *International Herald Tribune*, October 14-15, 1989; *U.S.S.R. Monitor*, no. 8 (Washington: The Heritage Foundation, March 1990); and *The Economist* (April 7, 1990), p. 64.
[46] The cynical description of the workers' deal with the government is: "We pretend to work and they pretend to pay."
[47] Snyder, "The Gorbachev Revolution," p. 125.
[48] Harry Gelman, cited in Breslauer, "All Gorbachev's Men," p. 99.
[49] On these developments see Fukuyama, *Gorbachev and the New Soviet Agenda*, pp. 23-26; Breslauer, "All Gorbachev's Men," pp. 95-97; and various press reports.
[50] On military group interests and changes in the military establishment see Meyer, "The Sources and Prospects of Gorbachev's New Political Thinking;" Fukuyama, *Gorbachev and the New Soviet Agenda*, pp. 28-30; Breslauer, "All Gorbachev's Men," p. 97; and, Daria Fane, "After Afghanistan: The Decline of Soviet Military Prestige," *The Washington Quarterly* 13, no. 2 (Spring 1990), p. 13.
[51] Albert L. Weeks, "The KGB: A Key Player in Kremlin Politics," *Defense & Diplomacy* 7, no. 10 (October 1989), p. 73.
[52] *Perestroika*, p. 43.

Chapter 4

[1] Oleg M. Derkovsky, "The Soviet Union and the Middle East: The Soviet Perspective," *Middle East Insight* 5, no. 4 (November/December 1987), p. 10.
[2] Igor Belaev, "Middle Eastern Conflicts and Proposed Solutions," *Mezhdunarodnaia Zhizn*, no. 5 (May 1988). The 1980 "crisis" refers to a purported American order to drop two nuclear bombs on northern Iran if Soviet forces invaded, though that obviously never happened. For some reason, Belaev ignores two potentially more serious crises in 1970: the intervention of Soviet combat forces against Israel during the War of Attrition, and the Syrian invasion of Jordan in 1970. Incidentally, the same Belaev (at least as reported in the October 10, 1987 edition of the Kuwaiti daily *al-Anba*), accused Israel of complicity in the attempted assassination of Pope John Paul II.
[3] Text in FBIS, *Daily Report: Soviet Union* (henceforth, FBIS-SOV), June 20, 1985, pp. H1-H2.
[4] For more on the reassessment of relations with Israel in the early Gorbachev era, see Galia Golan, "Gorbachev's Middle East Strategy," *Foreign Affairs* 66, no. 1 (Fall 1987), pp. 42-48; and, Yaacov Ro'i, "A New Soviet Policy Towards Israel?" *The Jerusalem Quarterly*, no. 44 (Fall 1987), pp. 3-17.
[5] James A. Phillips, "Gorbachev's 'Newthink' on the Middle East," *Midstream* 35 (August/September 1989), p. 13.
[6] *Jerusalem Post*, January 19, 1989.
[7] *Ha'aretz*, January 22, 1989.
[8] *Jerusalem Post*, January 24, 1990; *Izvestia*, January 25, 1990.
[9] *Ma'ariv*, June 5, 1990; *Voice of Israel*, in BBC, SWB, ME/0826 (June 26, 1990), p. A/7.
[10] *Ma'ariv*, January 15, 1989.
[11] *Ha'aretz*, March 30 and May 16, 1988.
[12] *Jerusalem Post*, January 31, 1990.
[13] *Ha'aretz*, May 19, 1988; *Ma'ariv*, May 23, 1988
[14] *Ma'ariv*, June 1, 1988; *Jerusalem Post*, December 4, 1988; and *Ha'aretz*, December 5, 1988.
[15] *Al-Dustour* (Amman), January 28, 1990.
[16] See for example *Perestroika*, p. 125; Gorbachev's statement to a western trade union delegation, cited in *Davar*, March 11, 1988; and the report of his meeting with Egyptian Foreign Minister Ismat Abd el-Magid, in *Ha'aretz*, May 23, 1988.
[17] *Izvestia*, April 27, 1989; *Radio Moscow*, cited in *The Jerusalem Post*, November 21, 1989.
[18] *Ha'aretz*, October 15, 1989; *Al-Ahram*, October 25, 1989.
[19] For the text of the statement, see *Pravda*, April 27, 1987, in *Current Digest of the Soviet Press*, 39, no. 17 (May 27, 1987); for the dinner remarks see Golan, "Gorbachev's Middle East Strategy," p. 41; *Ha'aretz*, April 24, 1987; and Michael Bar-Zohar, *Facing a Cruel Mirror*, as serialized in *The Jerusalem Post*, May 23, 1990.

[20] *Yediot Aharonot*, October 30, 1988; and *Jerusalem Post*, December 12, 1988.
[21] *Jerusalem Post*, March 28, 1989; *Economist Foreign Report*, April 6, 1989, pp. 2-3.
[22] *Washington Post*, November 20, 1989; *Ha'aretz*, January 19, 1990.
[23] Quoted in *Ha'aretz*, October 20, 1988.
[24] Hannah, *At Arms Length*, p. 32; *Jerusalem Post*, December 14, 1989.
[25] *Washington Post*, November 21, 1988.
[26] *Ha'aretz*, April 10, 1988; *International Herald Tribune*, April 11, 1988.
[27] *Ma'ariv*, September 18, 1988; *Yediot Aharonot*, October 14, 1988.
[28] See Hannah, *At Arms Length*, p. 19.
[29] *Ma'ariv*, October 23, 1990 and October 26, 1990.
[30] See, for example, the remarks of the Soviet charge d'affaires in Iraq in *The Jerusalem Post*, April 15, 1990.
[31] *Ukaz* (Jeddah), in FBIS-NES-90-150 (August 3, 1990), p. 6.
[32] *Radio Algiers*, in FBIS-NES-90-049 (March 13, 1990), p. 1.
[33] Cited in *The Jerusalem Post*, September 28, 1990.
[34] *Ruz al-Yusuf*, in FBIS-NES-90-080 (April 25, 1990), p. 4.
[35] *Jerusalem Post*, February 8, 1990.
[36] As part of his effort to promote Lebanese national reconciliation, Soviet Deputy Foreign Minister Gennadi Terrasov met Aoun in August 1989. *Jerusalem Post*, August 27, 1989.
[37] Atef Gawad, "How the Gulf was Won: Oil and Islam in Soviet Foreign Policy," *American-Arab Affairs*, no. 22 (Fall 1987), p. 60.
[38] *International Herald Tribune*, July 14, 1988; *TASS*, in BBC, SWB, ME/W0066m (February 28, 1989), p. A2; and, KUNA, in FBIS-NES-90-089 (May 8, 1990), p. 12.
[39] *Iraqi News Agency*, in FBIS-NES-90-146 (July 30, 1990), p. 23.
[40] Vladimir A. Isayev, "USSR, Iraq: Progress Report and Prospects for Bilateral Relations" (mimeo, 1991), p. 3.
[41] United States Information Service, *Official Text*, August 8, 1990.
[42] *International Herald Tribune*, August 18-19, 1990; United States Information Service, *Official Text*, September 19, 1990.
[43] On offers of help with transport (subsequently denied by Soviet spokesmen), see *International Herald Tribune*, September 18 and 19, 1990; on offers of data on Iraq, see interview with KGB Chairman Vladimir Kryuchkov, *International Herald Tribune*, September 20, 1990.
[44] "The War That Might Not Have Been," *Pravda* (February 28, 1991), in *Current Digest of the Soviet Press* 43, no. 9 (April 3, 1991), pp. 8-9.
[45] And once even in a joint statement by Bessmertnykh and Secretary of State Baker. Text in *New York Times*, January 31, 1991.
[46] *New York Times*, February 14, 1991.

[47] See, for example, Peter Schweizer, "What Are Those Soviet Military Advisers Still Doing in Baghdad?" *International Herald Tribune*, August 23, 1990.
[48] *International Herald Tribune*, August 31, 1990.
[49] *Ibid.*, September 4, 1990.
[50] Fukuyama, *The New Soviet Agenda*, pp. 42-43.
[51] *Far Eastern Economic Review*, July 4, 1985, p. 22.
[52] *Jane's Defence Weekly*, November 23, 1985, p. 1125.
[53] *Jerusalem Post*, August 19, 1986.
[54] *New York Times*, December 10, 1986.
[55] For detailed reconstructions of this period, see Janice Gross Stein, "The Wrong Strategy in the Right Place: The United States in the Gulf," *International Security* 13, no. 3 (Winter 1988/89), pp. 142-67; and, Thomas L. McNaugher, "Walking Tightropes in the Gulf," in Efraim Karsh (ed.), *The Iran-Iraq War: Impact and Implications* (London: Macmillan Press for the Jaffee Center for Strategic Studies, 1989), pp. 171-99.
[56] Fukuyama, *Gorbachev and the New Soviet Agenda*, p. 47.
[57] *New York Times*, October 3, 1987.
[58] *International Herald Tribune*, March 10, 1988.
[59] *Jumhuri-ye Eslami*, cited in BBC, SWB, ME/0212 (July 25, 1988), p. i(a). Vorontsov's offer was a fairly transparent effort to recall the success at Tashkent in 1965, when the Soviet Union mediated an end to the Indo-Pakistan war.
[60] Radio Tehran, in FBIS-NES-90-069 (April 10, 1990), p. 49.
[61] BBC, SWB, ME/0874 (September 20, 1990), p. 1.
[62] See reports in BBC, SWB, ME/0432 (April 12, 1989), p. A/8; *Christian Science Monitor*, April 12, 1989; and, *Ha'aretz*, April 16, 1989.
[63] International Institute for Strategic Studies, *The Military Balance*, 1985-86 and 1990-91; *The Gulf Crisis and the Superpower Summit: Prospects for Conflict Resolution*, Policy Review, no. 1 (Washington, DC: Middle East Insight, 1990), p. 13.
[64] On Soviet criticism of the accord, see Abraham Ben-Zvi, *Between Lausanne and Geneva: International Conferences and the Arab-Israel Conflict*, JCSS Study no. 13 (Tel Aviv: Jaffee Center for Strategic Studies, 1989), pp. 98-99.
[65] Gennadi Gerasimov, interview in *Ma'ariv*, October 21, 1988.
[66] Y. Dmitriyev, "The Palestine Resistance Movement at New Frontiers," *Mirovaya Ekonomika I Mezhdunarodnyye Otnosheniya*, no. 8 (August 1987), in JPRS-UWE-87-012 (19 November 1987), p. 29.
[67] *Middle East News Agency*, in FBIS-NES-90-045 (March 7, 1990), p. 19.
[68] Chodikoff, "Political Dimensions of Superpower Intervention," p. 35.
[69] *Pravda*, May 27, 1981, cited in Freedman, "Soviet Policy Toward Syria," p. 40.
[70] Ro'i, "A New Soviet Policy?" p. 9.
[71] Heikal, *The Road to Ramadan*, p. 171.
[72] Korn, "U.S.-Soviet Negotiations in 1969."
[73] Trofimenko, "The Third World and the U.S.-Soviet Competition," pp. 1038-40.

[74] *Ma'ariv*, May 31, 1985. The last condition presumably refers to Soviet opposition to the Husayn-Arafat Agreement.

[75] Alvin Z. Rubinstein, *Moscow's Third World Strategy* (Princeton: Princeton University Press, 1988), pp. 290-91.

[76] See for example Steven R. David, "Africa: Moscow's Dubious Investment," in "The Empire's New Clothes: Moscow and the Third World After Afghanistan," *The National Interest*, no. 12 (Summer 1988), p. 133.

[77] In addition to the Syrians and Egyptians, other major Arab debtors included Iraq (3.8 billion rubles), Algeria (2.5 billion), Yemen (1.8 billion), and Libya (1.7 billion). *Izvestia* (March 1, 1990), cited in *U.S.S.R. Monitor*, no. 8 (March 1990). At the time, the ruble was worth approximately $1.60 at the commercial exchange rate, $0.16 at the tourist rate, and $0.05-0.07 on the black market.

[78] *Washington Post*, October 18, 1990.

[79] USSR Embassy, *News Release*, no. 15 (Ottawa: January 30, 1991), p. 2.

[80] *New York Times*, February 14, 1991; Fuller, "Moscow and the Gulf War," p. 58.

[81] Lt.-Gen. V. Nikityuk, interviewed in *Izvestia*, August 16, 1990, in FBIS-SOV-90-161 (August 20, 1990), p. 18.

[82] Quoted in Adam B. Ulam, *Expansion and Coexistence: The History of Soviet Foreign Policy; 1917-67* (New York: Frederick A. Praeger, 1968), p. 54.

[83] See for example Mikhail Agursky, "A Tilt Toward Israel," *The Jerusalem Post*, August 15, 1989, and "The Powerful Soviet Pro-Arab Lobby," *The Jerusalem Post*, March 3, 1990. Agursky claims that the military and KGB actually favor better relations with Israel.

[84] See for example Vladimir Nosenko, in *The Jerusalem Post*, November 11, 1990, and *Ibid*., November 15, 1990, p. 20.

[85] *Moskovskoye Novosti*, August 26, 1990.

[86] *Pravda*, October 24, 1989, cited in Hannah, *At Arms Length*, p. 53.

[87] BBC, SWB, ME/0685 (February 10, 1990), p. A/5; *Ha'aretz*, February 27, 1990.

[88] *Ma'ariv*, July 4, 1990.

[89] *International Herald Tribune*, June 4, 1990.

[90] *Komsomolskaya Pravda*, April 4, 1990.

[91] *Ha'aretz*, July 15, 1990.

[92] *Davar*, March 28, 1990, in FBIS-NES-90-060 (March 28, 1990), p. 20.

[93] See John Hannah, "Not a Drop of Russian Blood," *The Jerusalem Report*, November 15, 1990, pp. 40-41.

[94] *Novaya Vremya*, August 24, 1990.

[95] A.I. Ginzburg, "Improvement of Nationality Relations in the Light of the Decisions of the 27th CPSU Conference," *Obshchestvennyye Nauki V Uzbekistane* November 25, 1986, in JPRS-UPA-87-006 (16 June 1987), p. 58.

[96] *Turkmenistan Kommunisti*, in JPRS-UPA-88-014 (April 8, 1988), p. 51..

[97] BBC, SWB, ME/0668 (January 22, 1990), p. i, ME/0672 (January

26, 1990), p. A/1; and *International Herald Tribune*, January 25, 1990.

[98] Some Armenians, by contrast, were convinced that Gorbachev was guilty of a pro-Azeri, pro-Muslim bias; their evidence was his wife's "Turkish" name--Raisa.

[99] A. Mursaliyev, "Saddam and Gomorrah," *Komsomolskaya Pravda* (January 26, 1991), in FBIS-SOV-91-021 (January 31, 1991), p. 13; Graham Fuller, "Moscow and the Gulf War," *Foreign Affairs* 70, no. 3 (Summer 1991), p. 68.

[100] *Izvestia*, January 30, 1990, in *Current Digest of the Soviet Press* 42, no. 5 (March 7, 1990), p. 7.

[101] For more details see Alexandre Bennigsen et al., "Part I: The Soviet Islamic Establishment as a Strategic Instrument," in *Soviet Strategy and Islam* (Basingstoke: Macmillan, 1989).

[102] On these details see *International Herald Tribune*, April 25, 1990; *The Jerusalem Post*, September 18, 1990; and *The Economist* (April 22, 1990), p. 56. For more general background, see Carol R. Saivetz, "Islam and Gorbachev's Policy in the Middle East," *Journal of International Affairs* 42, no. 2 (Spring 1989), pp. 435-44.

[103] The leaders of these republics refused even to take part in discussions about a referendum for a new union treaty. *New York Times*, April 25, 1991.

[104] Shevchenko, *Breaking with Moscow*, p. 346.

[105] Shevardnadze claimed that the decision to invade Afghanistan was taken by a narrow circle of top officials: Brezhnev, Defense Minister Ustinov, KGB Chief Yuri Andropov, chief ideologue Mikhail Suslov, President Alexei Kosygin, and Gromyko. He also admitted that Krasnoyarsk was an "open violation" of the ABM Treaty. *International Herald Tribune*, October 24, 1989. The denunciation of the invasion of Czechoslovakia was made at a meeting of Warsaw Pact leaders (apart from Romania's) in 1989 and read on Soviet television evening news. *International Herald Tribune*, December 5, 1989. On the SS-20s, see "Foreign Policy: Lessons of the Past," *International Affairs*, no. 6 (June 1989), p. 82. The Katyn forest charge was made by a Polish-Soviet commission of inquiry on April 13, 1990.

[106] Anatoli Golovkov, associate editor of *Ogonyuk*, in *Jerusalem Post*, August 2, 1990.

[107] Nikolai N. Spasov, "Old And New Features of the Middle East Conflict," *Mirovaya Ekonomika I Medzhdunarodnaia Otnoshenia*, no. 3 (March 1990), reprinted in JPRS Report UWE-90-007 (July 23, 1990), p. 33.

[108] According to Shevchenko, this calculation led anti-Semites to support freer emigration during the first round of the debate, in the early 1970s. *Breaking With Moscow*, p. 348.

[109] McNaugher, "Walking Tightropes," pp. 172-74.

[110] Author's interview with former Assistant Secretary of State Richard Murphy, March 31, 1989.

[111] Despite Congressional and Defense Department efforts to restrict exports on sensitive technology, especially to Iraq, pressure from the Department of Commerce persuaded the White

House, on July 1, 1990, to lift export controls on over 30 types of equipment and materials, many of them essential for producing nuclear warheads and long-range missiles. *The Philadelphia Inquirer*, September 16, 1990.

[112] *The Washington Post*, February 20, 1991.

[113] Martin Walker, "Desert Storm over Moscow," *Ibid*., February 24, 1991.

Chapter 5

[1] A.S. Becker and A.L. Horelick, *Soviet Policy in the Middle East*, R-504-FF (Santa Monica: The Rand Corporation, September 1970), p. 87.

[2] *Washington Post*, January 11, 1989; *Al-Bayan* (Abu Dhabi), cited in *Jerusalem Post*, June 17, 1990.

[3] *TASS*, in FBIS-SOV-90-029, February 12, 1990, p. 21.

[4] For a detailed discussion see Shlomi Elad and Ariel Merari, *The Soviet Bloc and World Terrorism*, Paper no. 26 (Tel Aviv: Jaffee Center for Strategic Studies, August 1984).

[5] *Moscow's Third World Strategy*, p. 241.

[6] A major part of Foreign Minister Shevardnadze's speech to Egypt's National Democratic Party during his February 1989 tour of the region was devoted to the destructiveness of Middle Eastern arms races and to the need for arms control agreements, especially for a nuclear- and chemical-free zone in the region, and for various other confidence building measures, such as a military risk-reduction center and short-notice inspections. *TASS*, in BBC, SWB, ME/0394 (February 25, 1989), pp. A/4-A/7.

[7] At the 1991 Paris Air Show, the Soviet minister of aircraft production reportedly offered to sell Israel advanced MiG-31 interceptors. *Globe and Mail*, June 21, 1991.

[8] M. Yusin, cited in *Ma'ariv*, August 6, 1990; *Novaya Vremya*, August 10, 1990. Belonogov's answer was that the Soviet Union should rethink its concept of military cooperation and draw the appropriate conclusions.

[9] *Time*, March 26, 1990, p. 20.

[10] In this sense, Soviet concerns are analogous to the hysterical American reaction following the discovery of a Soviet brigade in Cuba in the late 1970s.

[11] "On the Soviet-Arab Dialogue in Amman," *Novaya Vremya*, May 27, 1988.

About the Author

Mark A. Heller received his BA in Political Science and Economics at the University of Toronto and did graduate studies at Harvard University, where he earned an MA in Middle Eastern Studies and a PhD in Political Science. Since 1979, he has been Senior Research Associate at the Jaffee Center for Strategic Studies, Tel Aviv University. His publications include *A Palestinian State: The Implications for Israel*, *The Middle East Military Balance*, which he edited and coauthored from 1983 to 1985, and numerous monographs, book chapters, and journal articles on Middle Eastern political and strategic affairs. He also coedited *The Soviet-American Competition in the Middle East.*

JCSS Publications

JCSS Publications present the findings and assessments of the Center's research staff. Each paper represents the work of a single investigator or a team. Such teams may also include research fellows who are not members of the Center's staff. Views expressed in the Center's publications are those of the authors and do not necessarily reflect the views of the Center, its trustees, officers, or other staff members or the organizations and individuals that support its research. Thus the publication of a work by JCSS signifies that it is deemed worthy of public consideration but does not imply endorsement of conclusions or recommendations.

The Jaffee Center for Strategic Studies
Recent Publications in English

1991-1992 Subscription Series

Study no. 18 Mark A. Heller, *The Dynamics of Soviet Policy in the Middle East: Between Old Thinking and New.*

Study no. 19 Dore Gold, *Israel as an American Non-NATO Ally: Parameters of Defense-Industrial Cooperation.*

Study no. 20 Karen L. Puschel, *US-Israeli Strategic Cooperation in the Post-Cold War Era: An American Perspective.*

War in the Gulf: Implications for Israel
Report of a JCSS Study Group. Edited by Joseph Alpher.

The Middle East Military Balance 1990-1991
Edited by Shlomo Gazit; with Zeev Eytan.

1990 Subscription Series

Study no. 15 Dore Gold, ed., *Arms Control in the Middle East.*

Study no. 16 Aryeh Shalev, *The Intifada: Causes and Effects.*

Study no. 17 Aharon Klieman and Reuven Pedatzur, *Rearming Israel: Defense Procurement Through the 1990s.*

Books

Anat Kurz, ed., *Contemporary Trends in World Terrorism* (New York: Praeger/Greenwood, 1987).

Ephraim Kam, *Surprise Attack: The Victim's Perspective* (Cambridge: Harvard University Press, 1988).

Efraim Karsh, ed., *The Iran-Iraq War: Impact and Implications* (London: Macmillan, 1989).

The West Bank and Gaza: Israel's Options for Peace
and
Israel, the West Bank and Gaza: Toward a Solution
Reports of JCSS Study Groups. Coordinator: Joseph Alpher, 1989.